Measuring Disaster Preparedness

Books by Author

Primer on Indicator Development and Application (1990)

Development and Application of Indicators for Continuous Improvement in Surgical and Anesthesia Care (1991)

Development and Application of Indicators for Continuous Improvement in Perinatal Care (1992)

The Measurement Mandate: On the Road to Performance Improvement in Health Care (1993)

Development and Application of Indicators in Emergency Care (1993)

Lexikon: Dictionary of Health Care Terms, Organizations, and Acronyms for the Era of Reform (1994)

Clinical Performance Data: A Guide to Interpretation (1996)

The First 72 Hours: A Community Approach to Disaster Preparedness (Editor) (2004)

Measuring Disaster Preparedness

◆

A Practical Guide to Indicator Development and Application

By Margaret O'Leary

iUniverse, Inc.
New York Lincoln Shanghai

Measuring Disaster Preparedness
A Practical Guide to Indicator Development and Application

iUniverse, Inc.

For information address:
iUniverse, Inc.
2021 Pine Lake Road, Suite 100
Lincoln, NE 68512
www.iuniverse.com

ISBN: 0-595-31708-1 (pbk)
ISBN: 0-595-76887-3 (cloth)

Printed in the United States of America

A Worthy Goal:

> *"When you can measure what you are speaking about and express it in numbers, you know something about it, but when you cannot measure it, when you cannot express it in numbers, your knowledge is of a meager and unsatisfactory kind."*
>
> —Lord Kelvin

But:

> *...knowing begins and ends in experience; but it does not end in the experience in which it begins."*
>
> —C.I. Lewis[1]

---

1. From: *Statistical Method from the Viewpoint of Quality Control* by Walter A. Shewhart, p. 80, 1939, republished 1986 by Dover.

Contents

Preface ix

CHAPTER 1   What Is Community Disaster Preparedness? 1

CHAPTER 2   Performance Management 29

CHAPTER 3   Framework of Performance Measurement 37

CHAPTER 4   Characteristics of Indicators 47

CHAPTER 5   Indicator Development Process 69

CHAPTER 6   Reliability and Validity: The Indicator Testing
             Process 77

CHAPTER 7   Summarizing Indicator Data 82

CHAPTER 8   Variation in Data 100

CHAPTER 9   Factors Influencing Variation 112

Afterword 117

Glossary 119

Index 143

Preface

One of the best ways to improve disaster preparedness is to measure it. The purpose of this book is to teach community leaders and their staff members how to develop and apply measurement tools, called "indicators," to improve local disaster preparedness. State and federal leaders interested in measuring disaster preparedness at various levels, and citizens residing in local communities who want more information about how well their community is prepared for disaster, may also find this book useful.

Measuring Disaster Preparedness has been written for people who are relatively new to the performance-measurement field but who have some familiarity with the disaster-preparedness field. People who want to gain a better understanding of local disaster preparedness may benefit from first reading *The First 72 Hours: A Community Approach to Disaster Preparedness*, an anthology of essays and dialogues contributed by local leaders in DuPage and Kane Counties, Illinois, in 2003.

The best way to read this book is as part of a group charged with developing disaster-preparedness indicators for the community. This is particularly true for readers who have a fear of, distrust of, or indifference toward numbers.

Each chapter of *Measuring Disaster Preparedness* is indispensable to readers who want to reach the goal, which is the continuous improvement of disaster preparedness.

Chapter 1 argues that disaster preparedness is a community core competence. Five core processes comprise the core competence: hazard analysis, surveillance, warning, rehearsal, and logistics. These five core processes form the basis for subsequent indicator development. In this chapter, readers will find the definitions of community and disaster preparedness.

Chapter 2 describes the position of measurement in a performance-management framework whose components are measurement, assessment, and improvement. Readers will learn that measurement is a precondition for improvement lest people identify improvement targets that may be vague, grandiose, or outside their fields of influence and control. They will also learn the meaning of the axiom "If you can't measure it, don't do it."

Chapter 3 focuses on the three components of performance measurement: indicators, standards/guidelines, and a performance database. The chapter illustrates, with examples drawn from disaster-preparedness literature, how these three tools interlock. Readers learn that a community is not necessarily prepared simply because structures (e.g., an office, a coordinator, a plan) are in place.

Chapter 4 introduces the reader to existing theories about, and practical applications of, the indicator measurement tool. Readers will learn that the most powerful indicators are "continuous variable indicators."

Chapter 5 provides a step-by-step approach to convening an indicator-development team and highlights lessons learned by successful indicator-development teams. Chapter 6 addresses indicator and data reliability issues. Readers will learn in this chapter that data produced by indicators is useful only to the extent that it measures what it is supposed to measure.

Chapter 7 introduces the important notion of data variation, which is the inevitable output of any measured process. Data sets each have frequency distributions and central locations (averages) that serve as anchor points when comparing numbers across organizations and time.

Chapter 8 delves into the theory of common-cause and special-cause variation, the ingenious tools developed by Walter Shewhart and later popularized by W. Edwards Deming. Chapter 8 explains when and why the reader needs to react to observed variations in data. Readers will learn that tampering with (overreacting to) data only makes things worse.

Chapter 9 provides an overview of the techniques used to improve disaster preparedness once the decision has been made to act on data that is showing special-cause variation. The best people to ferret out underlying causes of variation are the subject matter experts who developed the indicators in the first place. The Afterword stresses the importance that readers incorporate a culture of measurement into their communities and professional lives.

Following each chapter is a summary of important points covered in the chapter, references used in the chapter, and a set of study questions and projects. The book concludes with a glossary of important terms relevant to measuring disaster preparedness.

Measuring Disaster Preparedness is a challenging little book. It is meant to be that way. It is not for the faint of heart, but neither is preparing for community survival following the severe social stress that defines disaster. Learning to measure disaster preparedness is the first step in building community resilience to disasters.

Margaret O'Leary
April 13, 2004

1

What Is Community Disaster Preparedness?

One of the most formidable challenges facing local communities today is learning to apply the concepts and methods of performance measurement to disaster preparedness. Performance measurement operates on the theory that objective performance data about important processes and outcomes—generated through the application of performance measures or indicators—can and should be used to identify performance variations. Analyses of these variations form the basis for identification of process improvement opportunities.

The Disaster Cycle and Disaster Preparedness

In 1978, Whitaker advanced an explicit four-phase typology for disaster planning as part of a project she undertook for the U.S. National Governors' Association. [1] The four phases are as follows:

1. *Mitigation*: the totality of measures undertaken before a disaster to permanently prevent or reduce future disaster impact (e.g., building codes and land-use regulations)

2. *Preparedness*: the totality of measures undertaken in anticipation of imminent disaster (e.g., hazard analysis, surveillance, warning, rehearsals, logistics)

3. *Response*: the totality of measures undertaken during and immediately after disaster impact to resolve crisis-time problems (e.g., damage assessment, debris removal, search-and-rescue efforts, emergency medical services)

4. *Recovery*: the totality of post-response measures undertaken to restore the community to normalcy (e.g., rebuilding homes, reopening local businesses). [2]

Disaster preparedness as defined above occurs at multiple levels: individual, household, organizational, inter-organizational, community, state, national, and international. [3] Numerous studies show that commitment to disaster preparedness at the community level is low in spite of communities being left "on their own" immediately after a disaster strikes. [4-6]

For example, a 1994 study of Michigan's local emergency-planning committees (LEPCs), which were created through federal legislation in 1986 following the Union Carbide Corporation chemical release debacle in Bhopal, India, showed that there was considerable variation in the degree to which LEPCs had completed disaster-preparedness tasks. Approximately 30% of LEPCs had conducted hazard analyses, 26% had developed site-specific emergency plans, and 15% had trained emergency-response personnel. [7]

Why is community support for disaster preparedness low? First, disasters are relatively infrequent in a given locality, which often leads to a false sense among community leaders and residents that they are, at least most of the time, safe. Second, the infrequency of disasters results in a lack of real-time disaster experience. Lacking this experience, people must imagine how events unfold in a disaster. Some people *underestimate* the magnitude of disaster demands on the community, which leads to unrealistic optimism. The under-estimators say, "We can handle it. Disasters are only big emergencies. We handle emergencies well every day." Other people *overestimate* the magnitude of disaster demands, which leads to unnecessary fatalism. The over-estimators say, "What's the use? I just hope it's over fast. It's God's will. What will be, will be." [8] Third, participants in disaster preparedness can become mired in conflict because of "PET"—politics, ego, and turf." [9] Individuals and groups erect barriers to protect professional autonomy, identity, ideology, and access to resources. [8, 10-11]

Defining Community Disaster Preparedness

A *disaster* is a state or condition that destabilizes a social system. Disaster manifests itself in the malfunctioning, disruption, or partial or total destruction of connections and communications between the elements of the social system. Communities require extraordinary countermeasures to reestablish stability in a disaster. [12]

Examples of disasters are earthquakes, infectious disease outbreaks, wildland fires, and nuclear power plant explosions that occur in areas populated by people. The earthquake, infectious disease outbreak, wildland fire and exploding nuclear power plant are *disaster agents*—that is, phenomena that cause disasters.

A near synonym for disaster agent is "hazard." A *hazard* is an extreme phenomenon that has the potential to harm human settlements. [13] Hazards are frequently classified according to their origins. Tornadoes, flash floods, thunderstorms, earthquakes, winter storms, and hurricanes are examples of *natural hazards*. Hazardous materials releases in fixed facilities and during transport, railway accidents, air accidents, nuclear attacks, and terrorist attacks are examples of *technological hazards*. The combination of a natural hazard and a technological hazard (e.g., a tornado strikes a hazardous materials storage site or a downed power line ignites a wildland fire during high winds) produces a *complex disaster*.

A *community* is a relatively complex and relatively permanent geopolitical entity (an entire city, village, incorporated town, county, or parish) that has defined legal boundaries (see Table 1.1).[14–16] From a sociobiological viewpoint, a community is an evolutionary adaptation that guarantees more independence to the individual without depriving the individual of the benefits of social life, which include the propagation of the species, migration, and mutual defense. [16]

Table 1.1
Typology of Social Interaction Systems

Degree of Permanence	Degree of Complexity			
	Low			*High*
Relatively permanent	Groups	Organizations	Communities	Societies
Relatively transitory	Gatherings	Emergent organizations	Synthetic organizations	Social movements

*Source: J. Eugene Haas and Thomas E. Drabek: *Complex Organizations: A Sociological Perspective* (New York: The Macmillan Company, 1973) 6.

Communities today have become increasingly complex. Technology-dependent subsystems (e.g., communication, transportation, banking, defense) interlock. Stress to one subsystem may affect another subsystem, making entire communities increasingly vulnerable to hazards. Individual structures in a large urban area may survive a disaster, but the area malfunctions because basic lifeline systems, such as water, sewage, energy, transportation, and communication, have been disrupted.

Core Competencies and Core Processes

Prahalad and Hamel have contributed important insights to the understanding of how people in organizations organize themselves to transform inputs (e.g., raw materials, labor, energy, capital) into outputs (goods and services). [17] The typical organization is a hierarchy of smaller units, each with its own internal hierarchy, reporting upward in a pyramidal configuration. "Tables of organization" are the pictorial representation of this pattern (see Figure 1.1).

Figure 1.1
Hospital Emergency Incident Command System*

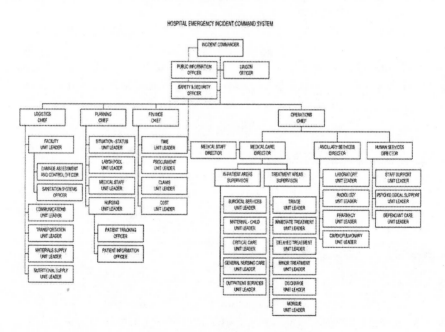

*Source: Emergency Medical Services Authority of California:
See http://www.emas.ca.gov/dms2/org2.htm

Prahalad and Hamel point out the perils of this hierarchical pattern and propose an alternative paradigm: a large tree, whose roots are "core competencies." Each core competence provides nourishment and stability to the trunk and major limbs (core processes), smaller branches (administrative units), and leaves, flowers, and fruit (goods and services). In this view, a community is anchored by its core competencies rather than its bureaucracy of administrative units.

A *core competence* is, according to Prahalad and Hamel, a social unit's "collective knowledge about how to coordinate diverse production skills and technologies."[17] An alternative definition of core competence is a social unit's unique areas of expertise, which distinguishes the social unit from others by providing value to users. Core competencies and the network of integrated processes that comprise them are so important to a social unit that they form the basis for ongoing performance measurement, assessment, and improvement activities. The three core competencies of the manufacturing giant 3M, for example, are substrates, coatings, and adhesives (i.e., sticky tapes). Core competencies of law enforcement include conflict resolution, use of force, and knowledge of statutes, among others. Two core competencies of emergency medicine are patient stabilization and disposition.

What are the core competencies of the city, village, town, county, or parish? What are the roots that keep these "trees" alive and strong as social forms? From the perspective of users (e.g., community residents), an important community core competence is disaster preparedness. A prepared community is more likely to demonstrate resilience (successful recovery) in the face of disaster.

What are the core processes (trunks, major limbs) of disaster-preparedness core competence? A *process* is a series of interrelated activities, actions, events, mechanisms, or steps that transforms inputs into outputs for a particular beneficiary or customer.[18] A *core process* is a process linked to a core competence. Five important core processes of disaster preparedness are

- Hazard analysis
- Surveillance
- Warning
- Rehearsal
- Logistics

Core Processes of Disaster Preparedness
Hazard Analysis

Hazard analysis is the process of quantifying the probability that extreme events will harm human settlements in a given geographic area during a specified period. Hazard analysis takes place at three levels of sophistication: 1) hazard identification, 2) vulnerability assessment, and 3) risk analysis. [19–20] A review of available county and state hazard analyses suggests variability in the conduct of hazard analysis (see Table 1.3). [21]

Table 1.2
Five Core Processes of Disaster Preparedness

Core Process	Definition
Hazard analysis	The process of quantifying the probability of extreme events harming human settlements in a given geographic area during a specified period.
Surveillance	The process of collecting, collating, and interpreting data to produce useful information.
Warning	The process of detecting imminent disaster and distributing that information to people at risk.
Rehearsal	The process of simulating a disaster for the purpose of measuring, assessing, and improving a social unit's future performance in a real disaster.
Logistics	The totality of resource-mobilization processes planned in anticipation of imminent disaster.

Table 1.3
Three Levels of Hazard Analysis

Name	Definition	Level of Sophistication
Hazard identification	The process of identifying what hazards have threatened a community, how often specified hazards have occurred in the past, and with what intensity (i.e., damage-generating attributes measured by various scales) they have struck.	Low
Vulnerability assessment	The process of quantifying the susceptibility of human settlements to the harmful impacts of hazards, including human death and injury, property damage, and indirect losses, such as interruption of business and production.	Medium
Risk analysis	The process of quantifying the probability that a hazard event will occur within a specified period.	High

Hazard identification (the first level of hazard-analysis sophistication) is the process of identifying what hazards have threatened a community, how often specified hazards have occurred in the past, and with what intensity (i.e., damage-generating attributes measured by various scales) they have struck.

Historical data is essential to hazard identification. For example, historical data in Clackamas County, Oregon, identifies the following hazards: earthquakes, winter storms (excluding flooding), hazardous materials (transportation-related and fixed-facility-related), volcanoes, flooding, terrorism, and landslides, among others. Four earthquake incidents (equivalent to a Level-2 emergency, *not* a worst-case scenario), one volcanic eruption, and one terrorist event have occurred in Clackamas County in the past one hundred years (see Table 1.4 and Table 1.7). [22]

Table 1.4
Definition of Three Emergency Levels, Clackamas County, Oregon*

Level	Definition	Examples	County Declaration?	Activation of EOC?**
1	An emergency incident that may be managed within the normal organization and procedures of emergency services agencies but may require specific notifications, the acquisition of unique resources (as requested by the on-scene incident commander), or coordination of specific activities to support the response.	Multiple patient incidents, second-alarm fires, severe weather with no power outages	Not usually	Not usually
2	An incident that has special or unusual characteristics requiring response by more than one agency or jurisdiction, the acquisition and use of specialized resources, or support to other jurisdictions, or which is beyond the scope of available county resources. Level-2 emergencies may require partial implementation of this plan, local declaration of emergency to access state resources or to enact emergency authorities, or notification and support as requested by the on-scene incident commander. Level-2 emergencies may be declared by the incident commander, the sheriff, the county fire defense board chief, the emergency management coordinator, or any public-safety official needing additional resources.	Critical disruptions of essential services for more than thirty minutes, mass casualty incidents, moderate to major hazardous materials incidents, and any evacuation expected to last more than four hours.	Probably not	Maybe
3	An incident that requires the coordinated response of all emergency resources at all levels of government to save lives and protect property during emergencies impacting a sizable portion of the county's population. Level-3 emergencies require implementation of the emergency-operations plan and may require declaration of an emergency to access resources to evacuate, shelter, or provide other lifesaving emergency services. Level-3 emergencies may be declared by the same individuals who declare Level-2 emergencies.	Train accident with hazardous materials, earthquake, major urban or wildland/urban interface fire, major flooding	Likely	Yes

*Source: Emergency Management, Clackamas County, Oregon:
see http://www.co.clackamas.or.us/emergency/
**EOC = emergency operations center

Vulnerability assessment (the second level of hazard-analysis sophistication) is the process of quantifying the susceptibility of human settlements to the harmful impacts of hazards, including human death and injury, property damage, and indirect losses, such as interruption of business and production. Hazards identified in Kane County, Illinois, include tornadoes, flash floods, floods, thunderstorms, and hazardous-materials spills, among others. Vulnerability assessment for a given hazard (e.g., floods) is based on the percent of population/property likely to be affected by a hazard event. For example, if greater than ten percent of the Kane County population is susceptible to a hazard, Kane County has a "high" level of vulnerability to the hazard (see Table 1.5). [23]

Table 1.5
Hazard Ranking, Kane County, Illinois*

Hazard	History	Vulnerability	Maxi-mum Threat	Probability	Overall Score
Tornado	High	High	High	High	High
Flash flood	High	High	Medium	Medium	High
Flood	High	High	Medium	Medium	High
Thunderstorm	High	Medium	Medium	High	High
Hazardous materials spill	High	Medium	Medium	High	High
Ice storm	High	High	Medium	Low	Medium
Railway accident	High	Medium	High	Low	Medium
Winter storm	High	Medium	Medium	Medium	Medium
Air accident	High	Medium	Medium	Medium	Medium
Earthquake	Low	High	High	Low	Medium
Hazardous materials storage accident	High	Medium	Medium	Low	Medium
High temperature/ insufficient rainfall	Medium	Medium	Medium	Medium	Medium
Nuclear attack	Low	High	High	Low	Medium
Terrorist attack	Low	High	High	Low	Medium
Dam failure	Low	Medium	High	Medium	Medium
Ice jams	High	Low	Low	Medium	Low
Gas interruption	Low	Medium	High	Low	Low
Industrial accident	Low	Medium	Low	Low	Low

*Each event was scored to identify high priority hazards. Each of the four criteria was assigned a numerical value depending on the rating (low, medium, or high). Since some criteria are considered to more important than others, a weighting factor was used to balance the total score. Source: Emergency Management Agency, Kane County, Illinois: see http://www.kcoem.org/

A second vulnerability assessment is sometimes performed using a worst-case scenario—that is, the worst conceivable destruction of life and property that a hazard event could cause. "Maximum threat" is the name given to this worst-case scenario. A "high" maximum threat-level rating means that the hazard in its most virulent form would affect greater than twenty-five percent of the population in a geographic area (see Table 1.5, column 4).

Risk analysis (the third and highest level of hazard-analysis sophistication) is the process of quantifying the probability that a hazard event will occur within a specified period. There are many ways to quantify risk level for hazards.

For example, "high risk" in both Kane and Clackamas Counties' hazard models means that one hazard incident will probably occur within a ten-year interval. "Moderate risk" means one hazard event will probably occur within a fifty-year interval. "Low risk" means that one hazard event will probably occur within a one-hundred-year interval. Clackamas County officials have assigned a high probability to the earthquake hazard, meaning that they expect one to occur within ten years (see Tables 1.6 and 1.7).

Table 1.6
Hazard-Analysis Criteria, Clackamas County*

Hazard	History: based on the number of times a hazard event has occurred in past 100 years. Weighting factor is 2.	Vulnerability: based on the percent of population or property likely to be affected. Weighting factor is 5.	Maximum Threat: based on the percent of population killed or injured or major infrastructure or property damage caused in worst-case scenario. Weighting factor is 10.	Probability: based on the likelihood of an occurrence within a specified period of time. Weighting Factor is 7.	Total Risk to Community: based on sum of weighted preceding factors.
Scoring: High=7–10 pts Moderate: 4–6 pts Low: 1–3 pts					
	High=4 or more events in last 100 years; moderate=3 events in last 100 years; low=1 or 0 events in last 100 years.	High=more than 10% affected; moderate=1–10% affected; low=less than 1% affected.	High=more than 25% could be affected; moderate=5–25% could be affected; low=less than 5% could be affected.	High=one incident within a 10-year period; moderate=one incident within a 50-year period; low=one incident within a 100-year period.	

*Source: Emergency Management, Clackamas County, Oregon: see http://www.co.clackamas.or.us/emergency/.

Table 1.7
Hazard Ranking List, Clackamas County, Oregon*

Hazard	History (W.F. = 2)	Vulnerability (W.F. = 5)	Maxi- mum Threat (W.F. = 10)	Probability (W.F. = 7)	Total Score
Earthquake	4	10	2	7	187 points
Winter storm	10	10	2	10	160 points
Hazardous materials, transportation	2	5	7	10	148 points
Volcano	1	9	7	2	131 points
Flood, tributaries	8	8	1	9	129 points
Terrorism	1	9	6	3	128 points
Landslide	10	2	1	10	110 points
Windstorm	4	6	2	6	100 points
Drought	4	10	1	4	96 points
Civil disorder	5	7	1	5	90 points
Dam failure	1	7	4	1	84 points
Transportation, air or rail	2	3	3	5	84 points
Power failure	2	9	1	2	73 points

*Source: Emergency Management, Clackamas County, Oregon:
see http://www.co.clackamas.or.us/emergency/.

An alternative method of calculating hazard probabilities is to estimate occurrence on an annual basis. This approach enables one to make estimations, for example, there is a ten percent chance of a Category-3 hurricane (Saffir/Simpson scale) striking a given county in any given year. A third way of expressing probability is as a recurrence interval, such as a 100-year storm (a storm with a 1 percent annual probability) or a 475-year earthquake (a 0.2 percent annual probability). Hazard maps often provide the basis for hazard identification and are available to the public online (on an advisory basis only). [24]

When all of the hazard-analysis data is scored and summed, a prioritized list of hazards in a community can be generated. The Kane County and Clackamas County Hazard Ranking Lists are presented in Tables 1.5 and 1.7, respectively. The hazard-prioritization process forms the basis for subsequent decisions concerning resource allocation to prepare for disasters.

Surveillance

Surveillance is the process of collecting and interpreting data to produce useful information. *Information* is data that has been transformed through analysis and interpretation into a form useful for drawing conclusions and making decisions.

The data has at least three important dimensions: time (temporal), geography (spatial), and quality (completeness, accuracy). Failure by degrees in one or more of the dimensions can render data useless or even harmful as a tool for performing other disaster-preparedness processes, such as warning.

The *time dimension* of data includes variables such as when the data is collected; the time interval required for the collection; and the lag time between when the data is collected, when it becomes available to users, and how frequently new data is collected. For example, thirty cities nationwide (February 2004 information) currently rely on biosensing filters to accurately detect up to fifteen potentially lethal airborne germs. Each filter requires twenty-four hours for processing to produce the usable information. [25] Germs spread rapidly, and hours can mean the difference between forestalling an epidemic and allowing it to take hold. In this scenario, the surveillance data may be accurate, complete, and specific to a city but lack usefulness because of the twenty-four-hour interval required to obtain the needed information.

The *spatial dimension* of data is characterized by variables such as scale, resolution, and extent. Hazard maps are used to depict the spatial relationships of entities and are extremely important in local disaster preparedness. Indeed, technological advances such as Doppler radar and remote-sensing technologies (e.g., weather satellites) have provided scientists, emergency practitioners, and private citizens with access to near-real-time surveillance images for many (but not all) types of hazards, including severe weather and wildfires.

The *quality dimension* of data is the degree to which collected data is accurate (i.e., free from errors) and complete (i.e., data exists and is available for use). The degree to which data is accurate and complete directly affects the reliability of the data and information derived from the data, which is used to make decisions.

Unreliable data is always invalid, meaning that it is useless for its intended purpose (e.g., hazard analysis, surveillance, warning). [26]

The Great Midwest Flood of 1993 illustrates the importance of data reliability. It severely tested national, state, and local means of managing natural resources and handling emergencies. A controversial aspect of the flood was the relatively poor quality of data (e.g., river levels, dates when crests would occur and when the flood would end) issued by the National Weather Service and the Army Corps of Engineers. [27] Many flow-measuring systems were damaged, destroyed, or rendered inoperable during the flood. Basic hydrologic models were incapable of generating reasonable outcomes, in part because they did not take into account levee failures, future precipitation, and changes to the basins as a result of human intervention. Poor quality data resulted in the need to constantly revise (increase) the assessments of flood damages (e.g., barge losses, crop losses, and flood losses), which, in turn, required additional political attention to recalculate federal and state relief aid. [27]

As of yet, no comprehensive database exists in the U.S. to provide all-hazards surveillance data. For example, data from natural hazards is collected separately from that of technological hazards. In addition, a plethora of public and private national, state, and local organizations collect data on a single type of hazard.

At the local level, real-time or near-real-time surveillance for imminent hazard events is critical to communities that are "on their own" for some time after disaster impact. As a result, communities need to invest in technologies that enhance their ability to locate data and information needed to support decision making in real-time or near-real-time. Hazard-surveillance data typically issues from many public and private organizations. The good news is that an increasing amount of natural-hazards data is available on the Internet. [28–29]

Warning

Warning is the process of detecting imminent disaster and distributing that information to people at risk. Warning is the oldest way of coping with disaster. The most effective warning systems integrate three subsystems: detection of extreme events, management of hazard information, and public response. The best warning systems currently exist for floods, hurricanes, and volcanoes. [30]

Warnings tend to be hazard specific, because hazards differ in the following six ways:

- Predictability (the degree to which a hazard can be forecasted well with respect to magnitude, location, and timing)

- Detectability (the degree to which predictions correlate well with the impacts that occur)

- Certainty (the level of confidence that detections will be accurate and not result in false alarms)

- Lead time (the amount of time between prediction/detection and the impact of the hazard)

- Duration of impact (the time between the beginning and end of impacts, in which warning information can be disseminated)

- Visibility (the degree to which the hazard physically manifests itself so that it can be seen or otherwise sensed) [31]

Warnings are notoriously difficult to develop for epidemics. Potentially lethal germs are invisible to the eye and other senses and are therefore difficult to detect until illness occurs. Germs can spread quickly over hours, meaning that an epidemic can take hold before it is possible to issue a warning.

Tornado warning systems, by contrast, have improved steadily over the past twenty years because of improvements in weather satellites, radar, training of forecasters, local storm-spotter networks, and awareness campaigns. [32] Models of how tornadoes form now use parent circulation (mesocyclone) at midlevels in thunderstorms. Watches, warnings, and advisories are produced by the National Storm Center in Norman, Oklahoma, and disseminated via National Weather Services stations throughout the U.S.

No warning system is one-hundred percent reliable. For example, on August 28, 1990, from 3:15 to 3:45 P.M., the strongest tornado in northern Illinois in more than twenty years struck the towns of Plainfield, Crest Hill, and Joliet in Will County. The tornado developed extremely rapidly and was not detected by the conventional radar systems in use. A more sensitive Doppler radar was offline because of a previous malfunction. The affected area was served by two emergency warning sirens. However, because official tornado spotters had not observed funnel clouds, the sirens were sounded only after the tornado began its destructive course through the town of Plainfield. Approximately 300 people were injured, 28 killed. [33]

Two national warning systems are the Civil Defense Warning System (CDWS) and the Emergency Alert System, which warn of enemy attack, accidental missile launch, and radioactive fallout. All commercial broadcast stations and cable companies are required to participate in the system. The National Oceanic and Atmospheric Administration (NOAA) developed "Weather Radio" to provide warnings of severe weather through commercially-available tone-alert radios. Broadcast stations exist around the country, each serving a forty- to sixty-mile radius. A third national warning system is the color-coded Homeland Security Advisory System, which advises communities of terrorist threat levels based on credible surveillance (intelligence) data.

The U.S. currently has no comprehensive national warning strategy or system that informs users about *all* hazards in all places. Instead, public warning practices are decentralized across different political subdivisions and the private sector. For example, the local municipality may warn residents about a contaminated drinking-water supply, the local emergency-management agency may warn residents about imminent tornadoes, the National Hurricane Center in Miami may warn citizens about imminent hurricane landfall, and the U.S. Department of Homeland Security may warn citizens about an elevated risk of terrorist attack.

Not all hazards have organized warning systems. For example, most communities with hazardous materials sites (manufacture, storage) do not have special warning systems. Existing systems, such as chemical factory sirens and dedicated telephone "hotlines," have been developed primarily by private companies and communities as cooperative efforts. Disaster researchers have demonstrated that in most hazardous-materials accidents, the prime responsibility for issuing a warning falls on local emergency responders, such as firefighters or police officers, who are the first to arrive to the scene of a spill, fire or explosion. First responders must determine the nature of the hazardous material, whether it is a threat, whether people need to be warned, and what people need to know. [34]

The public response to a warning system is a multi-step process, including hearing or seeing (if one is deaf) the warning, believing the warning is credible, confirming that the threat does exist, personalizing the warning to oneself and confirming that others are heeding it, determining whether protective action is needed, determining whether protection is feasible, determining what action to take, and then taking it. [35]

Rehearsal

Rehearsal is the process of simulating a disaster for the purpose of measuring, assessing, and improving a social unit's future performance in a real disaster. The assumption behind rehearsing is that future performance can be enhanced. One physician, whose hospital system was participating in a disaster rehearsal, said, "Most disaster exercises end after the emergency-services personnel transport the patients to the hospital. Today, we have doctors, nurses, and other hospital staff all being trained in how to sort patients out once they get here. We really need this kind of training. You wouldn't hand a musician some sheet music and say, 'I'll see you at the concert. I hope everything goes well.' No, there is such a thing as rehearsal. This is our rehearsal." [36]

Disaster-preparedness rehearsals—synonyms include exercises, drills, disaster exercises, and disaster drills—are conducted at multiple levels: individual, household, organizational, inter-organizational, community, state, national, and international. Each successive level requires an expanding framework of operational expertise. For example, TOPOFF 2, conducted over five days in May 2003, was an international-level (U.S. and Canada) "multi-agency, multi-jurisdictional, real-time, limited-notice WMD [weapons of mass destruction] response exercise, designed to better prepare senior government officials to effectively respond to an actual terrorist attack involving WMD. In addition, TOPOFF 2 involve[d] law enforcement, emergency management first responders, and other non-governmental officials. Short of an actual attack, such exercises are the best possible way to train responders, gauge preparedness, and identify areas for improvement." [37]

Disaster-preparedness rehearsals are frequently conducted to assess political subdivision emergency-operations plans. An *emergency-operations plan* is, according to the administrative code of the State of Illinois, "the written plan of a political subdivision describing the organization, mission, and functions of the political subdivision government and supporting services for responding to and recovering from disasters." [38]

Emergency-operations plans are often organized around *functions*. A function is a goal-directed interrelated group of processes. Examples of functions are direction and control, transportation, communications, public works and engineering, firefighting, information and planning, mass care and social services, resource support, health and medical, rescue, hazardous materials, utilities, and criminal-justice services. A function may combine several or many specific processes. For example, in Clackamas County, the public-works function includes damage assessment and debris removal; the communications function includes emergency information and warning, an emergency alerting system plan, an amateur radio plan, and disaster aviation; and the utilities function includes water, sewerage, and surface-water management, electric, telephone, and natural gas, and other fuels.

Disaster rehearsals are often, but not always, categorized into three types: tabletop, functional, and full-scale exercises. A *tabletop exercise* is, according to the State of Illinois Administrative Code, "a low-stress, non-time-pressured, discussion-based exercise of a minimum of four functions of the emergency-operations plan, including the direction and control function, held in the emergency-operations center, the incident-command post, or another suitable facility." An *emergency-operations center* is the physical location where leaders gather to make policy and strategic management decisions during a disaster or disaster exercise. [38]

A *functional exercise* is "a time-pressured exercise of a minimum of four functions of the emergency-operations plan, involving strategic and tactical decision making, including the direction and control function, activating the emergency-operations center or the incident-command post, or both." A *full-scale exercise* is "a time-pressured exercise of a minimum of six functions of the emergency-operations plan, involving strategic and tactical decision making, including the direction and control function, activating the emergency-operations center and incident-command post and deploying responders, equipment, and resources to the field." [38]

Disaster rehearsals are not restricted to the public sector. Since Y2K, the business sector has embraced "business continuity planning," of which "disaster recovery" is one aspect. Even small organizations back up their data and move it offsite on a regular basis. Larger organizations use disaster-recovery vendors, which collect and protect data and reserve a certain number of servers, telecommunication equipment, and business space at a "cold site." Client organizations can recreate their entire information-technology environments at the cold site, if needed, in the aftermath of a disaster. One British vendor says, "We know that over 70% of businesses fail to recover at their first rehearsal. Yet rehearsal is something we can predict and carefully prepare for; it will not even take us by surprise." When staff members complain about the time used up rehearsing disaster-recovery systems, the vendor responds, "We say that deriving the plan is worth 30% of survival points, but rehearsal of it adds the other 70%." [39]

Disaster recovery needs to be a critical part of every information-technology routine. One observer notes, "One of the most important times for disaster recovery in the U.S. was the Y2K effort. Many of us technicians put many hours into this effort. When the day came, it was anti-climactic, as everyone knows, because nothing really happened. But for us, that was a huge blessing. It was not until 9/11 that people understood the importance of what the Y2K effort accomplished. For example, it took several weeks and at least six major tests involving many, many people and many, many companies to test the back-up plan for the stock market as a part of Y2K planning. After September 11, within a week, we were able to pull the stock market back up. Had 9/11 happened two years earlier, I don't know how long it would have taken to get the stock market up and running again. Y2K made everyone think about how to recover business data and, more importantly, the issues that a company faces in a disaster." [40]

Logistics

Logistics is the totality of resource mobilization measures planned in anticipation of disaster—that is, the process of managing the flows of people, goods, services, information, and other resources between the point of origin and the point of need.

The discipline of logistics has existed for millennia. For example, logistics in the military "makes up as much as nine tenths of the business of war." [41] Alexander the Great was perhaps the first logistician, because he realized that supply was the basis of strategy and tactics. [42] Throughout history, wars have been lost because of the "tyranny of logistics." One modern soldier remarked,

> The more I see of war, the more I realize how it all depends on administration and transportation...It takes little skill or imagination to see *where* you would like your army to be and *when*; it takes much knowledge and hard work to know where you can place your forces and whether you can maintain them there. A real knowledge of supply and movement factors must be the basis of every leader's plan; only then can he know how and when to take risks with those factors, and battles are won only by taking risks. [41]

In the last quarter of the twentieth century, the commercial world began to invest in logistics. Logistics represented one of the most important sources of profitability to companies that had maximized efficiency of core processes, such as manufacturing. Further improvements in productivity (output/inputs) now depended on how companies interacted with their suppliers and how they got their products to market. A near synonym of logistics in the business world is "supply-chain management." [42] The three activities of logistics are demand management, supply management, and fulfillment management. (For further discussion of these, see below.) [43]

Humanitarian relief organizations, such as the International Red Cross and Oxfam (Great Britain), have recently embraced logistics as a means to better coordinate the annual flow of disaster-relief goods, services, and information from governments, foundations, individuals, and the private sector to victims of natural disasters, civil conflict, and war. Humanitarian logistics is defined as "the processes and systems involved in mobilizing people, resources, skills, and knowledge to help vulnerable people affected by natural disasters and complex emergencies." [44–45] Humanitarian logistics encompasses an integrated group of processes, including procurement, transport, tracking and tracing, customs clearance, local transportation, warehousing, and last-mile delivery. Logisticians must get the right goods to the right place at the right time, within the boundaries of a budget that has yet to fully materialize.

Recent terrorist attacks on U.S. soil have prompted interest in logistics as a means for civilian populations to prepare for all hazards. A term related to logistics in the civilian world, in the context of disaster preparedness, is "surge capacity" or "surge capability," meaning the potential for a community to respond effectively and efficiently to a sudden, transient increase in demand for specific requirements, such as water and hospital services.

The three main processes comprising logistics are demand management, supply management, and fulfillment management. *Demand management* in the context of disaster preparedness is the totality of goal-directed measures that influence a condition requiring relief. For example, transportation-demand management (also called mobility management) refers to measures that influence travel behavior (how, when, and where people travel). The purpose of these measures is to increase transport system efficiency and achieve specific objectives such as rapid throughput during disaster evacuation. Water, electrical, and information technology-demand management refer to measures that influence the use of existing capacity. The purpose of these measures is to use incentives or penalties to correct circumstances where unmanaged demand is likely to result or exceed the ability of the system to deliver.

To establish a logistics system, one must first identify demand requirements: how much of what is needed at the community level, when is it needed, and how will it need to get there? At this point in disaster-preparedness history, this task is often difficult, because the comprehensive databases required for forecasting and modeling disaster impacts on communities are in many cases only a few years old. Preparedness logisticians thus depend on disaster scenarios of varying intensity to project response needs and develop response capabilities. For example, in 1999, officials with the Department of Health and Human Services and the Centers for Disease Control and Prevention projected demand for smallpox vaccine (in an emergency) based on one vaccination/person for every person in the U.S. (based on U.S. census data). This projection was perhaps easier to make because of the natural history of smallpox among unimmunized populations, the relative ease with which smallpox vaccine production could be restarted by a pharmaceutical company, the availability of federal tax dollars to cover the cost of manufacturing and storing the vaccine, and the availability of population data.

Supply management involves the procurement of supplies, production planning, and inventory. Consider, for example, the demand-and-supply issues involved in developing the federal government's Strategic National Stockpile in 1999. On the demand side, officials used an all-hazards approach to produce and stockpile twelve fifty-ton "push packages"—containing antibiotics, chemical antidotes, antitoxins, life-support medications, intravenous administration, airway maintenance supplies, and medical/surgical items—in twelve strategic locations in the U.S. The Strategic National Stockpile is designed "to supplement and re-supply state and local public-health agencies in the event of a national emergency anywhere and at anytime within the U.S. or its territories," according to Robert Claypool, M.D., deputy director, Office of Operations, Security, and Preparedness, Department of Veterans Affairs. [46] This physician also detected a certain "cognitive dissonance in having a great pharmaceutical response without a platform on which to practice the medicine." [47]

On the supply side, the stockpiled pharmaceuticals are supposedly adequate to treat about a million people for infectious disease and a few thousand people for chemical events. The twelve push packages comprise twenty percent of the available inventory to the federal government, according to Mr. Steven Bice, director, Strategic National Stockpile, Centers for Disease Control and Prevention.[48] Eighty percent of the inventory is in vendor-managed warehouses, which means that the federal government has contracted with pharmaceutical corporations and prime vendors to house and rotate the product in order to keep it fresh. The federal government currently owns more doxycycline (an antibiotic) than any country in the world. [48]

Fulfillment management involves the transportation, distribution, and warehousing of supplies needed by end users. For example, if smallpox erupted in the U.S., the Centers for Disease Control and Prevention has millions of doses of smallpox vaccine to distribute. In June 2002, Bice said,

> We will store it and we will get it out the door in an unbelievably short period of time, if required. Should that response be required of us, we now have vaccine repositories—very sophisticated locations, sophisticated meaning scientifically sophisticated, and the science of logistics and the science of medicine combined to make these repositories very, very unique in the U.S. There are four repositories in the country with the ability to store vaccines. [48]

As of January 31, 2004, the total number of vaccine doses shipped to and released for use by individual states was 291,400 (see Table 1.8). In addition, the

CDC has developed detailed guidelines concerning smallpox vaccination distribution, storage, and security measures that are available for review on its website. [49]

Table 1.8
Total Number of Smallpox Vaccines Released, as of 1/31/04*

State/Program	Number of Vaccine Doses Released, COB 01/31/04	State/Program	Number of Vaccine Doses Released, COB 01/31/04
Alabama	10,000	Alaska	300
American Samoa	0	Arizona	500
Arkansas	11,000	California	10,100
Chicago	4,200	Colorado	1,800
Connecticut	6,500	Delaware	700
District of Columbia	5,000	Florida	24,000
Georgia	900	Guam	0
Hawaii	4,500	Idaho	1,000
Illinois	10,000	Indiana	2,900
Iowa	1,000	Kansas	3,000
Kentucky	4,200	Los Angeles	9,200
Louisiana	10,000	Maine	3,000
Marshall Islands	0	Maryland	6,000
Massachusetts	1,500	Michigan	6,700
Micronesia	0	Minnesota	4,500
Mississippi	5,600	Missouri	5,000
Montana	1,000	Nebraska	4,000
Nevada	1,500	New Hampshire	3,000
New Jersey	6,500	New Mexico	5,000
New York	8,000	New York City	3,500
North Carolina	7,500	North Dakota	2,000
No. Mariana Islands	0	Ohio	6,500
Oklahoma	700	Oregon	400
Palau	200	Pennsylvania	10,000
Puerto Rico	100	Rhode Island	1,200
South Carolina	7,800	South Dakota	4,300
Tennessee	10,000	Texas	30,000
Utah	1,500	Vermont	2,000
Virgin Islands	0	Virginia	10,000
Washington	4,000	West Virginia	2,500
Wisconsin	2,500	Wyoming	2,600
Total Number of Vaccine Doses RELEASED, COB 01/31/04			**291,400**

*Source: Centers for Disease Control and Prevention:
see http://www.cdc.gov/od/oc/meida/smallpox.htm.

Chapter 1 Summary Points

1. Communities are often "on their own" immediately after a disaster strikes, yet the commitment of many communities to disaster preparedness remains low.

2. Disaster is a state or condition that destabilizes a social system. Communities require extraordinary countermeasures to reestablish stability following a disaster.

3. A hazard is an extreme event that has the potential to harm human settlements.

4. Disaster preparedness is the totality of goal-directed measures undertaken in anticipation of a disaster.

5. A community is a relatively complex and relatively permanent geopolitical entity (an entire city, village, incorporated town, county, or parish) that has defined legal boundaries.

6. A core competence is a social unit's collective knowledge about how to coordinate diverse production skills and technologies. Core competencies and the network of integrated processes that comprise them are so important to a social unit that they form the basis for ongoing performance measurement, assessment, and improvement activities.

7. Disaster preparedness is a community core competence. Five core processes of disaster preparedness are hazard analysis, surveillance, warning, rehearsal, and logistics.

Chapter 1 Study Questions

1. Is disaster preparedness a core competence of your community? Why or why not?

2. List the disaster-relevant organizations in your community.

3. How often does your community hold a community-wide disaster simulation?

4. List the five highest-risk hazards in your community.

5. Develop three community-level disaster-preparedness core processes in addition to the five listed in this chapter.

Chapter 1 References

1. "Emergency Preparedness Project, Final Report," National Governors' Association, Washington, D.C., 1978.

2. E. L. Quarantelli, "Disaster Planning, Emergency Management and Civil Protection: The Historical Development of Organized Efforts to Plan and to Respond to Disasters" (Paper #301, Disaster Research Center, University of Delaware, 2000) 18.

3. K. J. Tierney, M. K. Lindell, and R. W. Perry, *Facing the Unexpected: Disaster Preparedness and Response in the United States* (Washington, D.C., John Henry Press, 2001) 27–80.

4. Dennis S. Mileti, *Disasters by Design* (Washington, D.C.: National Academy of Sciences, 1999) 218–219.

5. Tierney, *Facing the Unexpected*, 58.

6. P. H. Ross, J. D. Wright, and E. Weber-Burdin, *Natural Hazards and Public Choice: The State and Local Politics of Hazard Mitigation* (New York: Academic Press, 1982).

7. M. K. Lindell, and M. Meier, "Planning Effectiveness: Effectiveness of Community Planning for Toxic Chemical Emergencies," *Journal of the American Planning Association* 60 (1994) 222–234.

8. D. F. Gillespie, "Coordinating Community Resources," in *Emergency Management: Principals and Practice for Local Government* (Washington, D.C.: International City Management Association, 1991).

9. Larry Langston, "All Hazards, All Local: the Role of the Municipal Emergency Manager," in M. O'Leary (ed.) *The First 72 Hours: A Community Approach to Disaster Preparedness* (Lincoln: iUniverse Press, 2004) 336.

10. D. E. Wenger, E. L. Quarantelli, and R. R. Dynes, "Disaster Analysis: Police and Fire Departments" (DRC Final Project Report No. 37, Newark: Disaster Research Center, University of Delaware, 1989).

11. Mileti, *Disaster by Design*, 216–217. Mileti writes, "There is at most a general idea of how police and fire departments plan and for what types of tasks and events. It has been noted that police departments, especially smaller ones, tend not to devote much internal energy to disaster planning. When they do plan, police agencies tend to do so in isolation from other community organizations; few have adopted an inter-organization approach to disasters. The police appear to believe that disasters can be handled through the expansion of everyday emergency procedures. Fire departments have improved their preparedness levels and expanded their disaster- and crisis-related tasks beyond firefighting. In particular, they tend to be involved in planning for the provision of emergency medical services and for responding to hazardous materials emergencies. Nevertheless, like police departments, fire departments show a tendency to only plan internally."

12. E. L Quarantelli, *What Is A Disaster?* (London: Routledge, 1998) 61–62.

13. R. E. Deyle, S. P. French, R. B. Olshansky, et al, "Hazard Assessment: The Factual Basis for Planning and Mitigation," in R. J. Burby (ed.), *Cooperating with Nature* (Washington, D.C.: John Henry Press, 1998) 121.

14. E. J. Haas and T. E. Drabek, *Complex Organizations: A Sociological Perspective* (New York: The Macmillan Co., 1973) 6.

15. D. E. Wenger, "Community Response to Disaster: Functional and Structural Alternations," in E. L. Quarantelli (ed.), *Disaster: Theory and Research* (Beverly Hills, CA: Sage, Year) 17–49.

16. Petr Kropotkin, *Mutual Aid: A Factor of Evolution* (Boston, MA: Porter Sargent Publishing, 1914) 53.

17. C. K. Prahalad and G. Hamel, "The Core Competence of the Corporation," *Harvard Business Review* Vol no. (May/June 1990) page.

18. Joint Commission on Accreditation of Healthcare Organizations: *Lexikon* (Oakbrook Terrace, IL, 1994) 640.

19. J. J. Cohrssen and V. T. Covello, "Risk Analysis: A Guide to Principles and Methods for Analyzing Health and Environmental Risks" (Council on Environmental Quality, Washington, D.C., 1989) 6.

20. Deyle, "Hazard Assessment," 119–166.

21. Enter search words "county" + "hazard analysis" or see, for example: http://www.kcoem.org/hazard.pdf; http://www.co.clackamas.or.us/emergency/plan/section4.pdf; and http://www.sema.state.mo.us/hazard.htm; http://www.pcoem.org/current1.htm.

22. Emergency Management, Clackamas County, Oregon: see http://www.co.clackamas.or.us/emergency/.

23. Emergency Management Agency, Kane County, Illinois: see http://www.kcoem.org/

24. ESRI: see http://www.esri.com/hazards/makemap.html.

25. W. K. Rashbaum and J. Miller, "NYC Prepares for Potential Terrorism at Republican National Convention," *New York Times*, 15 February 2004, section.

26. Joint Commission on Accreditation of Healthcare Organizations: *Primer on Indicator Development and Application* (Oakbrook Terrace, IL) 39.

27. Stanley Changnon, "The Lessons from the Flood" in S. Changnon (ed.), *The Great Flood of 1993* (City: Westview Press, 1996) 300–319.

28. D. S. K. Thomas, "Data, Data Everywhere, But Can We Really Use Them?" in S. Cutter (ed.) *American Hazardscapes: The Regionalization of Hazards and Disasters* (Washington, D.C.: John Henry Press) 61–76.

29. M. E. Hodgson and S. L. Cutter, Mapping and the Spatial Analysis of Hazardscapes, in S. Cutter (ed.) *American Hazardscapes: The Regionalization of Hazards and Disasters* (Washington: John Henry Press) 37–60.

30. Mileti, *Disaster by Design*, 174–5.

31. Ibid, 197.

32. Ibid, 176.

33. CDC. Tornado Disaster—Illinois, 1990. *MMWR* 40(2);33-36, January 18, 1991.

34. E. L. Quarantelli, D. C. Hutchinson, and B. D. Phillips, "Evacuation Behavior: Case Study of the Taft, Louisiana Chemical Tank Explosion Incident" (Miscellaneous Report #34, Disaster Research Center, University of Delaware, May 1983). See http://www.udel.edu/DRC/miscreports.html.

35. Mileti, *Disaster by Design*, 191.

36. University of Maryland Medicine: see http://www.umm.edu/features/dril.html.

37. U.S. Department of State: see: http://www.state.gov/s/ct/rls/fs/2002/1219.htm.

38. Illinois General Assembly: see www.legis.state.il.us/commission/jcar/adminncode.

39. Oxford Continuity Group: see: http://www.oxfordcontinuity.co.uk/ and http:///www.churchill.ukcentre.com/oxcom/nestart.htm.

40. E. L. Woods, "The Importance of Business Continuity," in M. O'Leary (ed.), *The First 72 Hours: A Community Approach to Disaster Preparedness* (Lincoln: iUniverse, 2004).

41. Martin Van Creveld, *Supplying War: Logistics from Wallenstein to Patton* (Cambridge: Cambridge University Press, 1977) 231.

42. Donald Engels, *Alexander the Great and the Logistics of the Macedonian Army* (Berkeley University of California Press, 1980).

43. Sunil Chopra and Peter Meindl, *Supply Chain Management* (Upper Saddle River, NJ: Prentice Hall, 2001).

44. Ricardo Ernst, "The Academic Side of Commercial Logistics and the Importance of This Special Issue," in *Forced Migration Review* 18: *Delivering the Goods: Rethinking Humanitarian Logistics* (Oxford Uni-

versity, September 2003) 5.See: http://www.fritzinstitute.org/images/FI.pdfs/fmr18%20final.pdf.

45. Anisya Thomas, *Humanitarian Logistics: Enabling Disaster Response* (San Francisco) 3. See: www.fritzinstitute.org.

46. Centers for Disease Control and Prevention, Bioterrorism: see http://www.bt.cdc.gov/stockpile/index.asp.

47. Robert Claypool, in "Surge Capacity—Is It Time to Move Beyond 'Just-in-Time'?" (Proceedings from the U.S. Medicine Institute for Health Studies, June 17, 2002, Washington, D.C.) 27. See: http://www.usminstitute.org/content/surgeforum_transcript.pdf.

48. Steven Bice, "Surge Capacity," 5–7. See: http://www.usminstitute.org/content/surgeforum_transcript.pdf.

49. Centers for Disease Control and Prevention: see http://www.bt.cdc.gov/agent/smallpox/vaccination/distribtuion.asp.

2

Performance Management

Performance management is a framework for identifying opportunities for improvement through the use of performance indicators. Synonyms and near synonyms for performance management include continuous quality improvement (CQI), continuous improvement (CI), quality improvement (QI), total quality management (TQM), performance improvement (PI), and continuous performance improvement (CPI), among others. [1] The theories and methods to improve performance originated in industry, where they evolved from a set of management and statistical process control methods developed and applied by Walter Shewhart and other engineers beginning in the 1920s. (See Chapter 8.) [2]

The theory of performance management views a social interaction system and its complex processes as the appropriate focus of efforts to improve performance. Individuals who work within the boundaries of a specified social interaction system are viewed as basically "good"—that is, they wish to perform to the best of their ability. When individuals cannot give their best performance, or when errors occur, remedial actions are usually most appropriately directed at the process(es) or system(s) of social interaction, not the individual. Although individual competence and performance remain important, the performance of processes and achievement of outcomes are seen as the product of all governance, management, provider, and support subsystems comprising the social interaction system.

For example, police cadets were assigned to operate new planning software in the Pier 92 New York City emergency-operations center (EOC) in the days following September 11th. (The collapse of the World Trade Center towers had decimated the primary EOC on the twenty-seventh floor of 7 World Trade Center.) The cadets expressed unfamiliarity with some of the software's functions, as well as with requirements for interpreting and prioritizing information. Performance-management theory would point to improvement opportunities in management processes, such as orientation, training, and staffing levels, rather than in provider-competence issues. [3]

Performance-management theorists state that "every process produces information on the basis of which the process can be improved.[4] The five core processes of disaster preparedness discussed in Chapter 1—hazard analysis, surveillance, warning, rehearsal, and logistics—are so important to disaster outcomes that the processes need to be measured over time (i.e., monitored) for effectiveness, timeliness and other performance dimensions.

The ongoing monitoring of important processes and outcomes can provide information that will help identify opportunities to improve preparedness. Thus, data generated through use of reliable and valid performance indicators, are central to the continual improvement of disaster preparedness.

Disaster-preparedness processes, because of their complexity and dependence on evolving knowledge and technology, as well as their dependence on the knowledge and skills of individuals, can always be improved according to performance-management theory, even when high levels of performance appear to have been met. The end result of performance management is that attention is focused on making an entire system's processes and outcomes better by constantly adjusting and improving the system itself instead of searching out and getting rid of "bad apples" (outliers). Performance management stresses the need to improve, on a continuing basis, all the processes that affect outcomes.

The Relationship between Quality and Performance

Quality is a judgment proceeding from or taking place in a person's mind rather than in the external world. What is quality to one person may not be quality to another person. As such, judgments about quality are *subjective* and open to criticism about their degrees of reliability, validity, and usefulness in improving processes or outcomes.

Performance, on the other hand, by definition takes place before an audience. As such, performance can be objectively quantified and compared (using reliable and valid indicators) with other similar performances. Accurate, complete, and relevant performance data can provide users with *objective* evidence upon which quality judgments can be based.

The Three Components of Performance Management

The three interlinked components of performance management are performance measurement, performance assessment, and performance improvement (see Figure 2.1 and Table 2.1). *Performance measurement* is the quantification of processes and outcomes; it uses one or more dimensions of performance, such as efficiency or effectiveness. (See Chapter 4.) *Performance assessment* is the analysis and interpretation of performance-measurement data, with the goal of transforming it into useful information. Performance assessment involves, among other processes, the application of statistical tools and techniques to the data to provide summarized data, such as control charts, that may be used to make decisions regarding performance-improvement opportunities. (See Chapters 7 and 8.) *Performance improvement* is the study and continuous adjustment of processes to increase the probability of achieving desired outcomes. (See Chapter 9.)

Figure 2.1
Performance Measurement: Benefits and Barriers

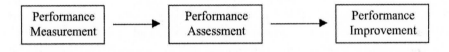

Table 2.1
Definitions of Performance Management Terms

Term	Definition
Performance management	The management approach that identifies opportunities for performance improvement through the use of performance indicators.
Performance measurement	The quantification of processes and outcomes, using one or more dimensions of performance, such as efficiency or effectiveness.
Performance assessment	The process by which data generated by performance-measurement activities is analyzed and interpreted.
Performance improvement	The continuous study and adjustment of processes to increase the probability of achieving desired outcomes.

Performance Measurement

Measurement has two meanings. First, it is the *process* of quantification—that is, determining that dimension of a process or outcome by which it is greater or less than the same dimension quantified for some other process or outcome. Each time someone counts the number of minutes between tornado warning and tornado impact, he or she is measuring (quantifying) a process. Second, measurement is the *number* resulting from the process of quantification. For example, a measurement of three minutes between tornado warning and tornado impact is the number resulting from quantifying the warning process.

Measurement permits conversion of important dimensions of processes or outcomes into quantifiable forms. Timeliness is an example of a quantifiable dimension of a process, such as tornado warning lead time.

Performance measurement is beneficial to communities for several reasons. First, it creates a common language based on numeric data. Together, these data constitute an immensely valuable set of numeric points of reference. The language of measurement enables communities, for example, to say, "Our average tornado warning lead time is three minutes. This number compares to the current statewide average of eleven minutes. Why is our lead time so low?"

Measurement creates the opportunity for a community to compare its numeric data for an outcome or process to its historical mean or some group average. The language of measurement is more than a new set of symbols consisting of numbers instead of words. The language of measurement changes the way people conceptualize and order their reality.

A second benefit of performance measurement is the ability to identify performance benchmarks. A benchmark is a point of reference or standard by which something is measured. Benchmarks of performance can be established for virtually any measurable process or outcome. The term "benchmarking" means to study someone else's processes and outcomes to learn how to improve one's own.

Benchmarking in disaster preparedness is important because communities cannot really know that their performance needs to be improved or has improved until they have actually measured it. The first measurement establishes a point of reference or baseline number for subsequent measurements. A second measurement, such as a group average from a database or a community's historical mean, can aid in determining whether improvement opportunities exist. A second measurement is also useful to ascertain the degree to which changes have resulted in improvements. One observer astutely noted, "For purposes of guiding decisions, improvement does not exist (in any useful way) until it is measured." [5]

A third benefit of measurement is that the measurement data can be used to set improvement priorities. Most communities quickly learn that there are many more improvement opportunities than can reasonably be addressed at a given time. Reliable performance data can help communities order and sequence their efforts in improving multiple performance areas.

A fourth benefit of measurement is its ability to improve the accuracy with which humans observe and record phenomena and form conclusions through data analysis about the observed phenomena. Ordinary human memory sensing—that is, use of the senses (e.g., sight, hearing) and memory as the sole bases on which to form conclusions and make decisions—is more subject to errors than when quantitative measurement is effectively conducted. Quantitative measurement is especially useful in addressing performance issues that may involve varying degrees of emotional overlay or deeply held beliefs. In these two situations, human senses are especially prone to error.

A fifth benefit of measurement is its ability to keep communities more clearly focused on concrete improvement opportunities. Improvement without measurement encourages people to identify improvement targets that may be vague, grandiose, or outside their fields of influence and control. A good rule for designing improvement projects is, "If you can't measure it, don't do it."

A sixth benefit of measurement is its ability to foster participants' acceptance of, and involvement in, the goals and processes of community disaster-preparedness improvement. The measurement process provides concrete feedback, which encourages people to take more active roles in improvement. When improvement goals are intangible ("Let's do better") and progress toward those goals is not adequately monitored ("Let's meet again in a few months to see how everyone is doing"), people tend to lose interest and, as a result, remove themselves mentally and/or physically from performance-improvement efforts.

Finally, measurement provides milestones toward which people can strive. Once reached, milestones provide an opportunity to celebrate. For example, in 1978, warnings were issued for only twenty-two percent of tornadoes, and the average lead time was three minutes. In 1995, those figures had risen to sixty percent and almost nine minutes. [6] These are important milestones that demonstrate the degree of improvement in tornado warning lead times achieved in a relatively short span of time.

Performance measurement can arouse concerns and fears, resulting in the erection of barriers that limit its ability to stimulate improvement in communities. One barrier to measurement is the fear of disclosing performance-measurement information. A second potential barrier to performance measurement is the requirement for resources, such as education and training, additional staff, and information systems.

A third potential barrier to measurement is fear or, distrust of, or indifference toward numbers. In 1937, medical statistician Sir Bradford Hill noted,

Statistics are curious things. They afford one of the few examples in which the use, or abuse, of mathematical methods tends to induce a strong emotional reaction in nonmathematical minds. This is because statisticians apply, to problems in which we are interested, a technique which we do not understand. It is exasperating, when we have studied a problem by methods that we have spend laborious years in mastering, to find our conclusion questioned, and perhaps refuted, by someone who could not have made the observation himself. It requires more equanimity than most of us possess to acknowledge that the fault is in ourselves. [7]

Individuals who cannot follow arguments couched in mathematical terms will have difficulty managing progress in the disaster-preparedness field in the twenty-first century. Mathematician Dennis Rosen noted,

All the sciences—the biological, medical, economic, and social ones, as well as the physical ones—are being pushed by international assault into more logical structures….Nearly all scientists are following the physicists and chemists in seeking analysis and prediction by quantified logical argument rather than by inference based on qualitative description. And their medium of communication is mathematics.[8]

There are three ways to address concerns about numbers during community performance measurement and assessment activities: 1) keep the mathematics simple, especially early on in the process, 2) be patient as most people will overcome their concern about numbers through education and regaining a familiarity with numbers and their usefulness, and 3) bring into the group people with a good feel for mathematics who are also good communicators and teachers to provide explanations, when needed.

Chapter 2 Summary Points

1. Performance management is a framework that identifies improvement opportunities through use of performance indicators.

2. Performance management views a social interaction system and its complex processes as the appropriate focus of efforts to improve performance.

3. Performance management states that every process produces information, on the basis of which the process can be improved.

4.   Performance management is composed of three interlinked components: performance measurement, performance assessment, and performance improvement.

5.   Measurement has two meanings: it is the *process* of quantification and the *number* resulting from the process of quantification. Measurement allows conversion of important attributes of processes or outcomes into quantifiable forms.

6.   Measurement is beneficial because it allows planners to set priorities, establish benchmarks of performance, increase the accuracy with which humans observe and record phenomena and form conclusions through data analysis, keep people focused on concrete improvement projects, foster participants' involvement in and acceptance of improvement processes, and create milestones towards which people can strive and afterward celebrate.

7.   Barriers to measurement include the fear of disclosing performance information, the need for resources to support the process, and the fear or distrust of numbers.

8.   Patience, keeping mathematics simple, and inviting good communicators (who are also numerate) will help to minimize barriers to measurement.

Chapter 2 Study Questions

1.   List three situations in which an individual was blamed for an undesirable outcome. Apply performance-management principles to determine whether opportunities to improve the outcome rested with the individual, the system, or both.

2.   Identify three performance benchmarks relevant to disaster-preparedness processes or outcomes in your community.

Chapter 2 References

1.   Joint Commission on Accreditation of Healthcare Organizations: *Lexikon* (Oakbrook Terrace, IL, 1994) 214.

2.   W. E. Deming, *Out of the Crisis* (Cambridge, MA: Massachusetts Institute of Technology Press, 1989).

3. K. Kendra and T. Wachtendorf, "Elements of Community Resilience in the World Trace Center Attack" (Paper #318, Disaster Research Center, 2002) 26–27.

4. D. M. Berwick, "Continuous Improvement as an Ideal in Health Care," *New England Journal of Medicine* 320 (1989) 53–56.

5. Joint Commission on Accreditation of Healthcare Organizations: *The Measurement Mandate* (Oakbrook Terrace, IL) 29.

6. Dennis Mileti, *Disaster by Design* (Washington, D.C.: National Academy of Sciences, 1999) 75.

7. Bradford Hill A., *Principles of Medical Statistics,* 9th ed. (New York: Oxford University Press, 1971) vii.

8. D. Rosen, *Mathematics Recovered for the Natural and Medical Sciences* (New York: Chapman and Hall, 1992) ix.

3

Framework of Performance Measurement

In a growing number of communities today, residents are demanding objective evidence about how well organizations and individuals perform disaster-preparedness processes. Until recently, most people believed and generally accepted that procedures, safeguards, and control devices designed to ensure community disaster preparedness were in place and worked most of the time.

However, blind acceptance, especially since 9/11, is giving way to heightened awareness that more information is needed about the level of community disaster preparedness. One observer notes, "The citizens of every community have a right to expect that their local governments are doing everything possible to prepare the community for a future disaster…In a post-9/11 world, citizens expect that their elected officials have taken the steps to see that citizens are as informed, prepared, and protected as possible." [1]

Current Approaches to Measurement of Community Disaster Preparedness

In the past, organizations and individuals interested in performance measurement have used two major approaches to measure performance: standards-based review and case-based review.

Standards-based reviews use pre-established structure- and process-oriented standards to focus attention on the factors that must be in place for good performance to result. *Standards* are statements of expectations that define a social unit's capacity to perform well. There are two types of standards commonly used in standards-based reviews: structural and process.

Structural standards pertain to the type, number, and characteristics of the resources of a social unit. For example, the State of Illinois, through the Illinois Emergency Management Agency (IEMA) Act, has established the following three structural standards with the expectation that political subdivisions will comply with them:

1. Each municipality with a population of over 100,000 [must have] an emergency services and disaster agency (ESDA) that has jurisdiction over and serves the entire municipality.

2. Each ESDA [must have] a coordinator who has been appointed by the principal executive officer of the political subdivision.

3. Each municipality that is not required to and does not have an ESDA [must have] a liaison officer designated to facilitate the cooperation and protection of the municipal corporation with the county ESDA in which it is located. [2]

Process standards identify activities that should or should not be done. To continue with the above example, the State of Illinois, through the Illinois Emergency Management Agency (IEMA) Act, has established the following process standards with the expectation that political subdivisions will comply with them:

1. ESDAs [must] conduct a hazard analysis for the political subdivision, assess vulnerabilities within the political subdivision, assess response capabilities of the political subdivision, identify shortfalls in response capabilities, and develop strategies to alleviate shortfalls, such as memorandums of understanding, mutual-aid agreements, and Good Samaritan agreements.

2. Each ESDA is required to create and continually update an emergency-operations plan.

3. Each ESDA is required to coordinate a biennial evaluated exercise of the emergency-operations plan through a tabletop or functional exercise, as well as a full-scale exercise every fourth biennial [every eight years]. [2]

In the past, standards-based reviews were considered among the best available methods for measuring performance. However, the recent demand for more detailed information on performance is rendering the sole use of this approach, as currently known and understood, inadequate. *The growing consensus is that one cannot presume that a process is being performed well simply because the capacity to perform the process exists.*

For example, one cannot assume that a process is being performed at a high level simply because a political subdivision has complied with structure and process standards, such as hiring an emergency coordinator, writing a plan, or performing the required number and type of disaster rehearsals. Compliance with structure and process standards is indeed essential to disaster preparedness (an emergency coordinator *is* necessary, and so is a plan and rehearsals), but now there is a keen interest in measuring how well the community performs the processes it is capable of providing. How timely *are* hazard warnings? How effective *are* tabletop exercises in preparing communities for disasters? Are the structures and processes required by the emergency-operations plan linked to better outcomes?

Case-based review involves applying previously acquired information and knowledge to another similar situation for the purpose of making decisions. For example, a disaster-exercise evaluator, after noting a particular performance situation in a disaster exercise, remembers an earlier disaster exercise with a similar situation. The evaluator uses the decisions made in relation to the previous disaster-exercise situation to help determine the decisions relating to the current disaster exercise.

Subjectivity and variable degrees of reliability are the two main problems with case-based reviews. Two people may differ significantly on their measurement of performance of the same process. As a result, the judgments required in a compliance-measurement process may be subjective, varying between judges and between cases. The advent of pre-established criteria to evaluate processes does improve the reliability of measurements. Nevertheless, the use of case-by-case judgments to measure performance, rather than looking at patterns and trends in aggregate data, has persisted.

Performance Measurement

A complete performance-measurement framework employs three interlinked and synergistic tools: indicators, guidelines/standards, and a performance database (see Figure 3.1 and Table 3.1).

Figure 3.1
Three Components of a Performance Measurement Framework

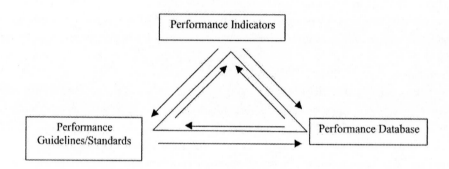

Indicators are measurement tools used to quantify performance of processes and achievement of outcomes. Indicators are not direct measures of performance. Rather, they are neutral screens that raise important performance questions that may lead one to identify governance, managerial, provider, and/or support processes in which opportunities for improvement exist. An example of a performance indicator is "Strategic National Stockpile deployment lead time during full-scale disaster exercises." Lead time is the time between the request for medical supplies from the stockpile and their arrival to the patient.

Table 3.1
Definitions of Performance Indicators,
Guidelines/Standards, and Database

Tool	Definition
Indicator	A measurement tool used to quantify performance of processes and achievement of outcomes.
Guideline	Standardized specifications for processes developed by a formal process that incorporates the best scientific evidence of effectiveness with expert opinion.
Standard	A statement of expectations that defines a social unit's capacity to perform processes well.
Database	A comprehensive collection of indicator data used to produce information to make decisions.

Guidelines are standardized specifications for processes developed by a formal process that incorporates the best scientific evidence of effectiveness with expert opinion. [3] Process specifications are developed for the "typical" hazard and "typical" circumstance and, therefore, may not apply to every disaster caused by a specified disaster agent in every situation.

Guidelines are often used to describe an appropriate and effective course of action. Guidelines usually focus on what should or should not be done to achieve desirable outcomes. Synonyms and near synonyms include policies, procedures, protocols, and algorithms.

The operations manual of the fire department of the City of Phoenix, Arizona, includes many good examples of community-wide guidelines for care of emergency medical system (pre-hospital) patients. [4] One guideline, for example, is "the process for involved facilities and agencies to effectively manage seasonal emergency department overloads." This guideline describes the appropriate and effective course of action for what emergency medical technicians (EMTs) and hospitals should do when a hospital's emergency department or trauma service is saturated with patients, or when a hospital is experiencing an internal disaster or equipment failure. [5]

Standards, as defined and discussed earlier in this chapter, are statements of expectations that define a capacity to perform processes well. The U.S. Environmental Protection Agency (USEPA), for example, regulates the safety of community drinking-water systems through standards-based reviews. These water systems currently provide drinking water to ninety percent of Americans. Through the Public Water System Supervision program, USEPA sets and enforces drinking-water standards that place limits on acceptable levels of contaminants. The limit for total coliform bacteria is five percent of samples in a month of collections. The National Primary Drinking Water Regulations (NPDWRs, or primary standards) are legally enforceable standards that apply to community public-water systems. [6]

Indicators and guidelines/standards serve two distinct purposes in performance measurement. These should not be confused. The purpose of guidelines and standards is to provide the basis for an appropriate and effective course of action. The purpose of indicators is to 1) determine the degree to which the course of action is actually followed and 2) determine the impact of following that course of action.

The City of Phoenix guideline for hospital overload situations mentioned above specifies three pre-hospital diversion conditions (a hospital with a saturated emergency department, a saturated trauma service, or an internal disaster or equipment failure). When one or more of these conditions is present, EMTs are expected to transport their *medically-stable* patients to another hospital. Two corresponding indicators would quantify 1) the degree to which hospitals and EMTs actually follow the guideline and 2) the impact of the diversionary process on patient outcomes.

In certain cases, indicators may reveal that guidelines, developed through expert consensus and literature-review processes, may not actually result in acceptable outcomes. For example, a municipality may discover (through a lawsuit, perhaps) that a medically-stable patient who was not taken to the nearest hospital (which was on diversionary status for an acceptable reason) experienced an undesirable medical outcome. In such a case, the guideline may require modification.

Organizations and individuals involved in performance measurement often develop guidelines and standards with the expectation that their use will be measured. Indeed, experience suggests that guidelines and standards are more readily incorporated into processes when the degree to which they are used *is* measured and when collected data is conveyed to providers and other relevant groups and individuals. The indicator tool can be so powerful that the process of developing, publishing, and distributing an indicator may push behavior in the desired direction.

Guidelines and standards may provide the basis for developing indicators and, conversely, indicators may provide the basis for developing or refining guidelines and standards. Sometimes, valid guidelines and standards cannot be developed *a priori* for certain processes because there is a lack of knowledge or expert consensus as to what constitutes appropriate and effective processes. In these instances, indicators can be developed and used to assess which course(s) of action results in the desired outcomes.

Consider, for example, that rapid movement of stockpiled antibiotics to patients is a desirable process during an outbreak of plague. Twenty percent of the cache of antibiotics exists in the twelve federal stockpiles located throughout the U.S. From these locations they are moved, via Department of Defense transportation, to their destinations. Eighty percent of the cache of antibiotics exists in pharmaceutical-vendor-managed "virtual stockpiles" that are distributed to their destinations via private distribution channels (logistics companies). [7] Which way is quicker—transporting antibiotics from the Strategic National Stockpile or from pharmaceutical vendor warehouses? Applying an indicator to the situation can provide the data to answer such questions.

Advances in knowledge may require that guidelines (or standards) and indicators be modified to reflect these advances, based on newer outcome performance data. For example, the incident-command system (ICS) is a widely-touted decision-making tool developed in California during the 1980s for very large multi-jurisdictional wildfire incidents.

The ICS imposes a consistent hierarchical organizational structure, task break-down, and terminology on a set of activities that have been known to show great variability across responding organizations, communities, states, and disaster events. The assumption underlying the ICS is that preplanning and well-understood lines of communication and responsibility yield better disaster management. *However, there has never been any systematic empirical research that confirms this assumption.* [8] In fact, disaster field researchers have long contended that ICS is a poor management model in times of crises. [9–11] The ICS guideline may require modification based on indicator data that measures ICS effectiveness during disaster.

The third essential tool of performance measurement is the creation of a *performance database.* This database is a comprehensive collection of data collected to produce information relating to performance. The creation of a performance database sets the stage for addressing important related issues. These include standardizing data-element definitions, determining which data elements to collect, and applying methods for ensuring data accuracy and completeness. These issues plague current databases and must be resolved to ensure the utility of and confidence in future disaster databases. [12]

A comprehensive disaster-preparedness database should eventually provide the capability to produce continuous and timely data feedback to social units concerning core processes and to identify areas where opportunities for improvement are most likely to exist. In addition, the database should provide the capability to monitor the utility of guidelines and standards through the use of indicator data and should make available the information necessary to permit the updating and refining of guidelines and standards.

Chapter 3 Summary Points

1. Since 9/11, the growing consensus is that one cannot presume a high level of performance simply because the capacity to perform exists.

2. The two traditional means of measuring performance are standards-based reviews and case-based reviews.

3. A complete performance-measurement framework employs three interlinked and synergistic tools: indicators, guidelines/standards, and a database.

4. Standards are statements of expectations that define a capacity to perform well.

5. Structural standards pertain to the type, number, and characteristics of resources.

6. Process standards identify activities that should or should not be done.

7. Performance indicators are tools used to measure processes and outcomes. Indicators are *not* direct measures of performance. Rather, they are neutral screens that are designed to raise important questions that may lead to identification of governance, managerial, provider, and/or support processes in which opportunities for improvement exist.

8. Guidelines are standardized specifications for processes developed by a formal process that incorporates the best scientific evidence of effectiveness with expert opinion.

9. Guidelines and standards are often developed with the expectation that their use will be assessed.

10. Performance indicators and guidelines/standards serve two distinct purposes in performance measurement. These should not be confused. The purpose of guidelines and standards is to provide the basis for appropriate and effective courses of action. The purpose of indicators is to determine the degree to which the courses of action are actually followed and their impact on disaster response outcomes.

11. A performance database is designed primarily to provide meaningful information concerning the performance of processes and the achievement of outcomes.

Chapter 3 Study Questions

1. What are the three components of performance measurement? How are they related?

2. How do indicators differ from guidelines?

3. What purpose do guidelines serve in performance measurement?

4. What purpose do indicators serve in performance measurement?

5. Identify three standards/guidelines relating to disaster preparedness in your community.

6. Develop corresponding indicators to the three standards/guidelines. (See #5 above.)

7. Identify an example of a case-based review relating to disaster preparedness in your community. Why is case-based review a less desirable method for quantifying performance?

Chapter 3 References

1. Larry Langston, "All Hazards, All Local: the Role of the Municipal Emergency Manager," in M. O'Leary (ed.) *The First 72 Hours: A Community Approach to Disaster Preparedness* (Lincoln: iUniverse Press, 2004).

2. State of Illinois' Joint Committee on Administrative Rules, Administrative Code, Title 29: Emergency Services, Disasters, and Civil Defense; Chapter 1: "Emergency Management Agency," Part 301: "Political Subdivision Emergency Services and Disaster Agencies," Subpart B: "Emergency Operations Plan Requirements," Sections 301.210–Section 301.260.

3. Leape LL: Practice guidelines and standards: An overview. *QRB* 16:43, 1990.

4. The Phoenix Fire Department:
see http://www.ci.phoenix.az.us/FIRE/start_here.html.

5. The Phoenix Fire Department:
see http://www.ci/phoenix.az.us/FIRE/2050a.html.

6. U.S. Environmental Protection Agency:
see http://www.epa.gov/safewater/mcl.html.

7. Bice, Steven in "Surge Capacity—Is It Time to Move Beyond 'Just in Time?'" Proceedings from the U.S. Medicine Institute for Health Studies, June 17, 2002, Washington, D.C., p. 5-7. See: http://www.usminstitute.org/content/surgeforum_transcript.pdf.

8. Tierney KJ, Lindell MK, Perry RW: *Facing the Unexpected*. National Academy of Sciences, 2001, pp 210-212.

9. Quarantelli EL: The *Questionable Nature of the Incident Command System*. http://www.semp.us/archives/biots/biot16.pdf, Aug. 9, 2002.

10. Kendra J, Wachtendorf T, Quarantelli EL: *Who Was in Charge of the Massive Evacuation of Lower Manhattan by Water Transport on 9/11? No Was One, But It Was an Extremely Successful Operation: Implications?* http://www.semp.us/archives/biots/biot23.pdf, Sept. 26, 2002.

11. Dynes RR: *Government Systems for Disaster Management*. Disaster Research Center, University of Delaware, 2000, Paper #300, p. 8.

12. Thomas DSK: "Data, Data Everywhere, But Can We Really Use Them?" in S. Cutter (Ed.): *American Hazardscapes*. National Academy of Sciences. 2001, pp 61-76.

4

Characteristics of Indicators

Each indicator possesses a number of characteristics that define and enhance its usefulness as a tool to measure performance. Each indicator measures a process or an outcome, a desirable or an undesirable event or phenomenon, and one or more dimensions of performance. The dimensions of performance include appropriateness, availability, coordination, effectiveness, efficacy, efficiency, private citizen perspective issues, safety, and timeliness.

In addition, each indicator collects and aggregates data about many events or phenomena, or a single serious event that always requires further investigation each time it occurs. Finally, indicators possess measurable degrees of reliability and validity that determine their usefulness in identifying areas for improvement. The development of an indicator information set for each indicator helps users acquire clear dimensions about the indicator.

Outcome vs. Process Indicators

An indicator measures either an outcome or a process (see Table 4.1). An *outcome indicator* measures what happens or does not happen depending on how well one or more processes are performed. An *outcome* is the cumulative effect at a defined point in time of performing one or more processes.

"Terrorist acts committed by foreign national(s) against U.S. interests within U.S. borders" is an outcome indicator. The outcome is a terrorist act. The terrorist act is a result of the degree to which processes designed to prevent the terrorist act have been performed well.

A *process indicator* measures an interrelated series of activities, actions, events, mechanisms, or steps that transform inputs into outputs for a particular beneficiary or customer. "Strategic National Stockpile deployment lead time during full-scale disaster exercises" is a process indicator. As discussed in Chapter 3, lead time is the time between the request for medical supplies from the stockpile and their arrival to the patient. A series of steps transforms the request (the input) into the arrival of supplies where needed (the output).

The best process indicators focus on processes that are closely linked to outcomes, meaning that a scientific basis exists for believing that the process, when performed well, will increase the probability of achieving a desired outcome. For example, there is scientific evidence linking education and training to provider (e.g., firefighter, police officer, health professional, emergency manager) competence. In the Strategic National Stockpile example immediately above, scientific evidence exists linking availability of medical resources (e.g., antibiotics for an epidemic) to health outcomes, such as morbidity and mortality.

Process indicators may also be useful—or may be the only type of indicator whose use is feasible—when an outcome related to the process is difficult to measure for one or more reasons such as its rarity or occurrence at some distant time. For example, a terrorist act committed by foreign national(s) against U.S. interests within U.S. borders is a (hopefully) rare outcome and one that may occur long after the implementation of processes designed to minimize its occurrence. In such a case, measuring processes (linked to the outcome) with process indicators is more useful than measuring the outcome itself. Examples of processes linked to this outcome include 1) identifying and securing key assets in the U.S., 2) training more first responders, 3) training more bomb technicians, and 4) aggressively investigating computer intrusions. [1]

Table 4.1
Types of Indicators

Indicator Name	Definition	Example
Outcome indicator	An indicator that measures what happens or does not happen depending on the degree to which one or more processes are performed well	Terrorist acts committed by foreign national(s) against U.S. interests within U.S. borders
Process indicator	An indicator that measures an interrelated series of activities, actions, events, mechanisms, or steps that transform inputs into outputs for a particular beneficiary or customer	Strategic National Stockpile deployment lead time
Desirable indicator	An outcome or a process indicator that measures a desirable activity or result	First responders vaccinated against smallpox
Undesirable indicator	A process or an outcome indicator that measures an undesirable activity or result	Smallpox vaccine adverse reactions among first responders
Aggregate data indicator	A performance indicator based on collection and aggregation of data about many events or phenomena	Terrorist cases investigated
Continuous variable indicator	An aggregate data indicator that measures a continuous variable	Strategic National Stockpile deployment lead time
Discrete variable indicator	An aggregate data indicator that measures a discrete variable	Tornado warning lead time of less than nine minutes
Rate-based indicator	Same as discrete variable indicator	Tornado warning lead time of less than nine minutes
Sentinel event indicator	A performance indicator that identifies a serious individual event or phenomenon that triggers further analysis and investigation each time the event or phenomenon occurs	Terrorist acts committed by foreign national(s) against U.S. interests within U.S. borders

Desirable vs. Undesirable Indicators

Each indicator measures an event or phenomenon that is either *desirable* or *undesirable*. "Private citizens certified in community emergency response training" and "firefighters trained as hazardous-materials first responders" are examples of desirable events that indicators may quantify. "Hazard surveillance equipment downtime" is an example of an undesirable event that an indicator may measure.

Dimensions of Disaster-Preparedness Performance

Dimensions of disaster preparedness that indicators may measure include appropriateness, availability, coordination, effectiveness, efficacy, efficiency, private citizen perspective issues, safety, and timeliness. (See Table 4.2.) Indicators may be used to measure one or more of these dimensions for processes and outcomes.

Table 4.2
Dimensions of Performance Indicators May Measure

Indicator Performance Dimension	Definition
Appropriateness	The degree to which the correct process is performed, given the current state of knowledge
Availability	The degree to which process outputs are capable of being used, given the current state of knowledge
Coordination	The degree to which a process is performed in congruent action across communities, organizations, providers and time
Effectiveness	The degree to which a process is performed in the correct manner, given the current state of knowledge
Efficacy	The degree to which a process accomplishes what it is designed to accomplish
Efficiency	The ratio of the results of a process to the resources used to perform the process
Private citizen perspective issues	The degree to which individuals who live or work in a community are involved in the decision-making process in matters pertaining to disaster preparedness, and the degree to which they are satisfied with the disaster-preparedness services that they receive
Safety	The degree to which the hazard risk in the environment is reduced for private citizens, providers, organizations, and the community
Timeliness	The degree to which a process is performed at the time it is most beneficial or necessary

Appropriateness is the degree to which the correct process is performed, given the current state of knowledge. Conducting a community-specific hazard analysis, performing ongoing hazard surveillance, and rehearsing disaster simulations are appropriate processes, given the current state of knowledge. Two indicators that measure the appropriateness dimension of processes are "firefighters trained as hazardous materials first responders" and "public drinking water contamination notification lead time."

Availability is the degree to which process outputs are capable of being used, given the current state of knowledge. For example, hazard surveillance data is useless if it is not available to issue timely warnings. Warnings are useless if they are not available to citizens. Examples of indicators that measure the availability dimension of processes are "hard-of-hearing persons with alternative assistive technologies for severe weather warnings" and "tornado warning lead time."

Coordination is the degree to which a process is performed in congruent action across communities, organizations, providers, and time. For example, disaster logistics (moving resources such as personnel, water, food, fuel, medical therapeutics rapidly from one place to another) depends on the degree to which processes are performed in congruent action across communities, organizations, providers, and time. Examples of indicators that measure the coordination dimension of processes are "tornado warning lead time" and "cycle time from collection to distribution of local performance data to the public."

Effectiveness is the degree to which a process is performed in the correct manner, given the current state of knowledge. An indicator that measures the effectiveness dimension of smallpox vaccination process is "smallpox vaccine adverse reactions among first responders."

Efficacy is the degree to which a process accomplished what it has been designed to accomplish. An inefficacious service is almost always inappropriate. Examples of indicators that measure the efficacy dimension of disaster-preparedness processes are "Strategic National Stockpile deployment lead time during full-scale disaster exercises" and "floodplain residents with flood insurance."

Efficiency is the ratio of the results of a process to the resources used to perform the process. Efficiency is linked to appropriateness and effectiveness. For example, an ineffective process (that is, one not performed in the correct manner) or an inappropriate procedure (that is, a procedure that was performed incorrectly) will often result in wasted resources (inefficiency). Examples of indicators that measure the efficiency dimension of disaster-preparedness processes are "Strategic National Stockpile deployment lead time during full-scale disaster exercises," "hazard surveillance equipment downtime," and "disaster warning system cost (in dollars) to lives saved as a result of warning systems."

Private citizen perspective issues refers to the degree to which individuals who live or work in a community are involved in the decision-making process in matters pertaining to disaster preparedness and the degree to which they are satisfied with the disaster preparedness services that they receive. Examples of indicators that measure the private citizen perspective are "private citizens certified in community emergency response training" and "private citizens with household disaster plans."

Safety is the degree to which the hazard risk in the environment is reduced for private citizens, providers, organizations, and the community. Examples of indicators that assess safety from hazards are "terrorist cases investigated," "terrorist cases convicted," and "bomb technicians trained."

Timeliness is the degree to which a process is performed at the time it is most beneficial or necessary. Examples of indicators that measure timeliness are "hazard warning lead time" and "Strategic National Stockpile deployment lead time."

Individual indicators are not limited to assessments of a single dimension of performance. Rather, they are most often used to measure several dimensions of performance, because the dimensions of performance are often interlinked. The indicator "hazard warning lead time," for example, may measures effectiveness and availability dimensions of this process—that is, an unexpectedly high number of average minutes may be traced to availability issues (for example, communication equipment failures) and effectiveness issues (for example, provider competence issues).

Aggregate Data vs. Sentinel Event Indicators

Indicators are either aggregate data indicators or sentinel event indicators. (See Table 4.3 and Figure 4.1.) An *aggregate data indicator* is an indicator based on the collection and aggregation of data about many events or phenomena. A *sentinel event indicator* (discussed below) identifies serious isolated events.

Figure 4.1
Indicator Relationships

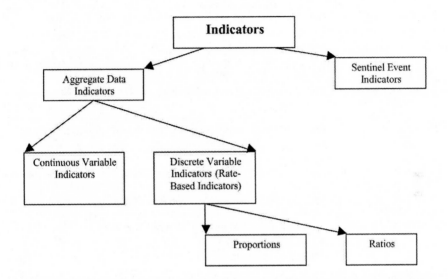

Source: Joint Commission on Accreditation of Healthcare Organizations, *The Measurement Mandate* (Oakbrook Terrace, IL: JCAHO, 1993) 128. Reprinted with permission.

Aggregate data indicators may be developed to measure either a discrete variable or a continuous variable. A *discrete variable* is a variable that, when measured, is limited to distinct options (for example, yes *or* no *or* unknown; less than or equal to five minutes *or* greater than five minutes). (See Table 4.3.) Thus, an aggregate indicator that measures a discrete variable classifies an event according to whether it falls into one discrete category or another, e.g., the event occurs *or* does not occur, or the event takes more than five minutes *or* less than five minutes.

Table 4.3
"Discrete" vs. "Continuous" Definitions

Term	Definition
Discrete data	Data that can be arranged into naturally occurring or arbitrarily selected groups or sets of values, as opposed to continuous data, which has no naturally occurring breaks
Discrete variable	A variable that, when measured, is limited to distinct options (for example, yes/no/unknown; less than 20 minutes or greater than 20 minutes)
Discrete variable indicator	An aggregate data indicator in which the value of each measurement is expressed as a proportion or as a ratio. Synonym: rate-based indicator
Continuous data	Data with a potentially infinite number of possible values along a continuum, e.g., minutes between hazard detection and impact
Continuous variable	A variable that, when measured, has a potentially infinite number of possible values along a continuum, e.g., minutes between tornado warning and tornado impact
Continuous variable indicator	An aggregate data indicator in which the value of each measurement can fall anywhere along a continuous scale

An aggregate data indicator that measures a discrete variable is commonly called a *rate-based indicator* (*discrete variable indicator* is also acceptable). Examples of rate-based indicators are "floodplain residents with flood insurance," "hearing-impaired persons owning alternative assistive technologies for hazard warning," and "firefighters trained as hazardous-materials responders." *Discrete variable data* is expressed by indicators that are founded on classifying items, such as events or phenomena, into at least two categories.

When using a discrete variable indicator, data is usually presented as a *ratio* or a *proportion*. A ratio is the relationship between two quantities when the numerator and denominator measure different phenomena. A *proportion* is a type of ratio, in which the numerator is expressed as a subset of the denominator.

An example of a discrete variable indicator that expresses indicator data as a proportion is: "floodplain residents with flood insurance," or

<u>floodplain residents with flood insurance</u>
floodplain residents.

An example of a discrete variable indicator that expresses indicator data as a ratio is "warning system cost per life saved as a result of warning system," or

<u>annual disaster warning system cost (dollars)</u>
lives saved as a result of warning systems (lives)

A *continuous variable*, when measured, has a potentially infinite number of possible values along a continuum such as time. An aggregate data indicator that measures a continuous variable is called a *continuous variable indicator*, e.g., "tornado warning lead time."

The actual values for each continuous variable (e.g., the time, in minutes; the weight, in pounds) are recorded and monitored over time using statistical process control techniques. As explained in Chapter 8, actions are taken to eliminate special causes of variation, which are factors that intermittently and unpredictably induce variation over and above that inherent in a system. Data that is expressed by continuous variable indicators is called *continuous variable data*.

Which indicator type is more useful—a continuous variable indicator or a rate-based indicator? The general consensus is that indicators that measure continuous variables and, thereby, generate continuous variable data, are more powerful than those measures built on discrete data. Continuous variable indicators are more powerful because data they generate contain more information and since additional statistical techniques can be used to assess the data.

Rate-based indicators measure an event for which a certain proportion of the events that occur represent expected performance. Therefore, further investigation is usually required only when the rate at which the event occurs becomes significant or certain trends or patterns in data over time are identified. (See Chapter 7, 8.)

Sentinel Event Indicators

A *sentinel event indicator* identifies a serious individual event or phenomenon that triggers further analysis and investigation *each time* the event or phenomenon occurs. While denominators may be identified for sentinel event indicators, these denominators ordinarily do not guide the decision as to when to review cases, because by definition a single occurrence of the event should trigger immediate review, whether the denominator is one or one thousand. An example of a sentinel event indicators is "terrorist acts committed by foreign national(s) against U.S. interests within U.S. borders."

In the past, sentinel events were associated with rare, adverse, and frequently avoidable events. Currently, however, sentinel events may occur with some frequency, depending on what indicator developers determine is an event that is serious enough to warrant further investigation each time it occurs. For example, humans can become infected with anthrax by handling products from infected animals, breathing in anthrax spores from infected animal products (e.g., wool), or eating undercooked meat from infected animals. But because anthrax was used as a terrorist weapon in fall 2001, occurrence of *any* case of human anthrax is now a sentinel event, meaning that each occurrence warrants in-depth investigation for bioterrorism.

Indicator Reliability and Validity

Each indicator possesses certain attributes that together determine its utility as a performance measure. Two key attributes are reliability and validity. Reliability and validity exist in measurable degrees. The goal is to develop indicators with the highest possible degrees of reliability and validity.

Indicator reliability is the degree to which the indicator accurately and completely identifies occurrences from among all cases at risk of being indicator occurrences. (See Table 4.4.) Indicator reliability is affected by false positive occurrences and false negative occurrences. Indicator events erroneously identified as occurrences are false positives. False positives inflate indicator rates (for rate-based indicators) and may overstate the need for response to the data. True indicator events that are erroneously unidentified as such are false negatives. They may result in artificially low indicator rates (for rate-based indicators) that may fail to trigger needed response to data. Indicators are developed with the intention of minimizing false positive and false negative occurrences.

Table 4.4
Indicator Reliability and Validity Definitions

Term	Definition
Indicator reliability	The degree to which the indicator accurately and completely identifies occurrences from among all cases at risk of being indicator occurrences
Indicator validity	The degree to which indicators identify events that merit further review
Face validity	Intelligibility or the degree to which an indicator makes sense, or appears to be a reasonable reflection of some variable, to an informed user

Indicator validity is the degree to which indicators identify events that merit further review. For example, an indicator that measures the American Red Cross' tornado warning lead time is an invalid indicator, because the American Red Cross does not issue tornado warnings. By contrast, an indicator that measures the American Red Cross' shelter set-up lead time is a valid indicator, because the American Red Cross *does* have control over the event the indicator is measuring.

During the initial development of an indicator, one often lacks the research to empirically establish whether an event, once reliably identified (i.e., once the data is complete and accurate), merits further review. Thus, as a practical matter, most development processes must depend on "face validity." *Face validity* is intelligibility, or the degree to which an indicator makes sense or appears to be a reasonable reflection of some variable, to an informed user. Face validity is the most superficial type of validity; nevertheless, it often contributes to the presumed legitimacy of an indicator and is, therefore, an important consideration in gaining acceptance of an indicator.

Reliability and validity are distinct but interlinked attributes of indicators. Unreliable indicators will almost always be invalid indicators. For example, if data collection is poor, an indicator cannot reliably point to opportunities for improvement and will therefore be invalid.

Reliable indicators, however, may not necessarily be valid indicators. For example, in the American Red Cross indicator example above, data about tornado warning lead time may have been collected in the correct manner, but if the American Red Cross does not participate in the warning process, the reliable data is useless for pointing to opportunities for improvement. Acceptable degrees of both reliability and validity are essential for indicators to be useful to communities.

Indicator Information Set

Indicator-specific information sets guide the development of indicators. The rationale behind developing indicators in this way is that examination of common indicator-related issues occurs prior to indicator testing and test data evaluation. The indicator information set invariably increases the subsequent utility of the indicator to users in their efforts to improve the performance of processes and achievement of outcomes.

The basic information needed to use an indicator includes 1) an indicator statement, 2) definition of terms, 3) indicator typology, 4) indicator rationale, 5) description of the indicator population, 6) indicator data collection logic, and 7) delineation of underlying factors that may explain variations in indicator data. (See Table 4.5.)

Table 4.5
Indicator Information Set Definitions

Term	Definition
Indicator information set	Indicator-specific information developed for each indicator to clarify issues and increase indicator utility
Indicator statement	Indicator information set component that describers the process or outcome being measured
Definition of terms	Indicator information set component that explains terms used in the indicator statement
Indicator typology	Indicator information set component that identifies whether the indicator 1) measures a process or an outcome or 2) is an aggregate data indicator or a sentinel event indicator, and, if it is the former, whether it is a discrete variable indicator or a continuous variable indicator, and, if it is a discrete variable indicator, whether it expresses data as a proportion or a ratio
Indicator rationale	Indicator information set component that explains why an indicator is useful in specifying and monitoring a particular process or outcome of disaster preparedness
Indicator population	Indicator information set component that describes an indicator's numerator and denominator; populations may be subcategorized to provide more homogeneous populations for subsequent data assessment
Indicator data collection	Indicator information set component that explains the sequence of data aggregation through which the numerator events and denominator events are identified by the indicator
Delineation of potential underlying factors	Information set component that delineates citizen-, provider-, organization-, community-, state-, and federal-level characteristics that may explain variations in performance data and thereby direct performance improvement activities and efforts

Indicator Statement

The *indicator statement* describes the process or outcome that is undergoing measurement by the indicator. Statements vary in their complexity. Some may be simple, such as: "Arbovirus detection following flooding." [3] Others may be complex because a variety of important qualifiers are introduced, e.g., "Community public water system with two consecutive coliform-contaminated water samples at one site in the same month and one of the samples is also fecal coliform positive or *E. coli* positive." [2]

Definition of Terms

The third component of the indicator information set is the *definition of terms* used in the indicator statement. Precise definitions will increase the probability that everyone using the indicator is collecting and assessing the same data. When terms are not precisely defined, the collection of comparable data and their meaningful analysis is difficult and sometimes impossible.

Lack of definitional precision is unfortunately common. For example, one study of 355 firms showed a relative lack of agreed-upon definitions between trading partners for the four most important logistical performance measures—on-time delivery, order fill, invoice accuracy and order cycle time (see Table 4.6). Indicators will be more useful if there is better agreement on definitions.

Table 4.6
Defining Logistical Performance Measures [4]

Measure	% Jointly Defined	% Customer Defined	% Neither
On-time delivery	31	29	40
Order fill	25	33	42
Invoice accuracy	28	30	42
Order cycle time	25	25	50

Indicator Typology

Indicator typology identifies 1) whether the indicator is an aggregate data indicator or a sentinel event indicator and, if it is the former, whether it is a discrete variable indicator or a continuous variable indicator, and, if it is a discrete variable indicator, whether it expresses data as a proportion or a ratio, and 2) whether the indicator measures a process or an outcome. (See Figure 4.1.)

For example, consider the indicator "first responders vaccinated against smallpox." This indicator is an aggregate data indicator, because it is based on the collection and aggregation of data about many events (one event being one first responder receiving a smallpox vaccination). Of the two types of aggregate data indicators (discrete variable and continuous variable), this indicator conforms to the discrete variable type, because it measures two discrete options (that is, a first responder is either vaccinated *or* not vaccinated). In addition, this indicator expresses data as a proportion:

$$\frac{\text{first responders vaccinated against smallpox}}{\text{first responders}}$$

Finally, this indicator is an outcome indicator, because it measures the result (a vaccinated individual) of the logistical cascade of interlinked processes responsible for moving smallpox vaccine from federal or state stockpiles to the end user (the vaccinee). Analyzing the indicator typology is important because this determination sets the focus for indicator data evaluation and use.

Indicator Rationale

The *indicator rationale* explains why an indicator is useful in specifying and monitoring a particular process or outcome of disaster preparedness. By stating the rationale for an indicator, those users considering the indicator gain a deeper understanding of its potential value and can better judge its merit (i.e., its face validity). During the early phases of indicator development, such rationales should be drawn from supporting literature references to the extent that these exist.

For example, the rationale for the indicator "first responders vaccinated against smallpox" might go as follows: First responders (e.g., medical professionals, public health officials, medical laboratorians, police, emergency medical technicians, firefighters) are a high-risk group for contracting smallpox in the event of its covert intentional release. Pre-exposure vaccination confers immunity in most people. First responders are critical community (human) resources. First responders need to be vaccinated to help the community during a smallpox crisis.

The indicator rationale should identify supportive references used to develop the indicator and identify the dimensions of performance measured by the indicator.

Description of the Indicator Population

The next component of the information set is a *description of the indicator population*—that is, the indicator's numerator and denominator—for rate-based indicators. In the cases of continuous variable indicators and sentinel event indicators, the indicator population is the numerator alone.

Indicator populations may be subcategorized depending on the attributes of the thing that is being monitored by the indicator. The purpose of subcategorizing is to provide more homogeneous populations for further analysis. For example, consider the indicator "hurricane warning lead time, subcategorized by Categories 1-5 (Saffir/Simpson scale)." In this indicator, the subcategories for further analysis are Categories 1, 2, 3, 4, and 5 (Saffir/Simpson scale).

Indicator Data Collection Logic

Indicator data collection logic is the sequence of data aggregation through which the numerator events and denominator events are identified by the rate-based indicator. Terms used in the indicator are translated into specific data elements, and corresponding data sources are identified by which data elements may be retrieved. Sample indicator data collection logic is presented in Table 4.7 for the indicator "annual eligible first responders vaccinated against smallpox, subcategorized by type of first responder."

Table 4.7
Sample Indicator Collection Logic for "Annual Eligible First Responders Vaccinated against Smallpox, Subcategorized by Type of First Responder."

Data Elements (Required by Indicator)	Data Sources
1. First responder = yes and	1. Local government and private sector human resource department records
2. Eligible to receive vaccination = yes and	2. Employee health record, medical record
3. Received smallpox vaccination = yes and	3. Public health record, employee health record (hospital, fire department, police department, independent laboratory, private ambulance company, mortuary coroner, medical examiner)
4. Between January 1, 2004, and January 1, 2005 = yes and	4. Public health record, employee health record (hospital, fire department, police department, independent laboratory, private ambulance company)
5. Subcategorized by Hospital-based clinicians Ambulatory care center-based clinicians Law-enforcement officers Firefighters Emergency medical technicians Public health clinicians	5. Hospital employee health record, ambulatory care center employee health record, fire department employee health record, police department employee health record, public health department employee health record

Delineation of Potential Underlying Factors

Delineation of potential underlying factors is the indicator information set component that describes citizen-, provider-, organization-, community-, state-, and federal-level characteristics that may explain variations in performance data and thereby direct performance-improvement efforts.

Private citizen factors include age, sex, illness, and disabilities that may contribute to the frequency of the event an indicator is measuring. Private citizen factors are usually not within the control of providers, organizations, or communities. Potential private citizen factors for the indicator "private citizens trained in certified emergency response training (CERT)," include old age, young age, and illnesses and disabilities. Citizen factors are usually acceptable explanations for variations in indicator data. For example, CERT indicator rates for a jurisdiction with a large concentration of elderly people in custodial care may be understandably low compared to other communities in which these two attributes are not factors.

However, one must clearly delineate private citizen factors to avoid misinterpreting the data—that is, attributing unexpected variations in data solely to private citizen factors when, in fact, provider, organization, community, state, and federal causes may also contribute to the observed variation. For example, a low CERT indicator rate in a community with a large concentration of Spanish-speaking citizens may not reflect the willingness and ability of Spanish-speaking citizens to learn emergency response techniques but rather the failure of the community to provide the CERT training in Spanish.

In addition, citizen factors may be modified by providers, organizations, or the community. For example, the probability that hearing-impaired citizens receive tornado warnings may be increased through assistive technology provided by organizations or the community.

Provider factors that contribute to variation in indicator data are usually controllable and are among the objects of thorough ongoing performance management. Because they are potentially controllable, provider factors usually point to opportunities for improvement (for example, through education and/or changing responsibilities).

Provider factors may contribute to indicator occurrences generated by the following indicator: "tornadoes correctly predicted with respect to magnitude, location, and timing, subcategorized by forecaster." Examples of potential provider factors that may help to explain variation in predicting tornadoes include forecaster level of initial training, continuing education, experience, disability, and illness.

Organization factors may contribute to variation in indicator data. For example, the need to address identified provider competence issues may also draw attention to the need for the organization to improve its credentialing and continuing education processes. Organization factors are usually controllable and are the object of a thorough monitoring process. In the indicator "tornadoes correctly predicted with respect to magnitude, location, and timing, subcategorized by forecaster," indicator occurrences may be attributed to a number of organization factors, such as the availability of surveillance equipment.

Community factors may contribute to the general ability of organizations to perform processes and achieve outcomes. These factors often point to opportunities for improvement in the horizontal and vertical integration of processes. Horizontal integration involves multiple disaster-relevant organizations, such as the police and fire departments, the American Red Cross, public health agencies, and local hospitals. Vertical integration involves municipal, county, state, and federal levels.

Community factors are usually controllable and are the object of a thorough measurement process. Common community factors that may help to explain indicator data include leadership capability, funding issues, and turf battles.

State and federal factors may contribute to the frequency of the event an indicator is measuring. State and federal factors are usually not within the control of providers, organizations, or communities.

Indicator Development Form

The information captured through development of the indicator information set is documented on an indicator development form. (See Figure 4.2.) Indicator information sets tend to undergo constant revision during the indicator development process. (See Chapter 5.) The multiple drafts of the indicator development form for each indicator provide an important historical document and need to be carefully labeled, tracked, and filed for future reference.

Figure 4.2
Sample Indicator Development Form

I. Indicator statement

II. Definition of terms

Define terms contained in the indicator statement that need further explanation for data collection purposes.

III. Type of indicator (circle correct answer)

a. Aggregate data indicator?	Yes	No
1. Rate-based type?	Yes	No
a. Proportion type?	Yes	No
b. Ratio type?	Yes	No
2. Continuous variable type?	Yes	No
b. Sentinel event indicator?	Yes	No

IV. Rationale

>a. Explain why this indicator is useful and the specific process or outcome that it will measure.

>b. Identify supportive references used to develop the above rationale.

>c. Identify the dimensions of performance measured by this indicator.

V. Description of the indicator population (rate-based indicators only)

>a. Indicator numerator:
>Indicator denominator:

>b. Subcategories (identify subpopulations by which the indicator data will be separated for analysis).

VI. Indicator data collection logic

>a. List the data elements and corresponding data sources from which data elements may be retrieved.

>b. Describe the sequence of data element aggregation through which the numerator events and denominator event for rate-based indicators only are identified by the indicator.

VII. Underlying factors

List factors that may explain variation in indicator data and thereby direct performance improvement activities.

a. Public citizen factors (factors outside the control of providers, organizations and the community that contribute to private citizen outcomes)

i. Age, sex, refusal to consent

ii. Illness

iii. Disabilities

b. Provider factors (factors, usually controllable by organizations, related to specific professionals, e.g., firefighters, emergency physicians and nurses, police officers).

c. Organization factors (factors, usually controllable by the organization, that contribute to either specific aspects of disaster preparedness or to the general ability of providers to provide disaster-preparedness services).

d. Community factors (factors, usually controllable by the community, that contribute to either specific aspects of disaster preparedness or to the general ability of providers and organizations to provide disaster-preparedness services).

e. State and federal factors (factors usually outside the control of providers, organizations, and communities).

Chapter 4 Summary Points

1. Indicators are quantitative tools designed to measure performance of processes and outcomes.

2. There are two types of indicators: aggregate data indicators and sentinel event indicators. An aggregate data indicator quantifies a process or an outcome related to many cases, as opposed to isolated cases, as in a sentinel event indicator. Aggregate data indicators are further subdivided into continuous variable and discrete variable indicators.

3.   Discrete variable indicators are commonly called rate-based indicators and may express information as a ratio or as a proportion.

4.   Rate-based indicators measure an event for which a certain proportion of the events that occur represent expected performance. Therefore, further investigation occurs only when the rate at which the event occurs becomes significant or certain trends or patterns in data are identified.

5.   Indicators may measure one or more dimensions of performance: appropriateness, availability, coordination, effectiveness, efficacy, efficiency, private citizen perspectives, safety, and timeliness.

6.   Indicators measure a process or an outcome. The best process indicators measure events or processes that are closely linked to outcomes. Process and outcome indicators may measure an event that is either desirable or undesirable.

7.   Indicators, to be useful, must possess reasonable degrees of reliability and validity. Indicator reliability is the degree to which the indicator accurately identifies occurrences from among all cases at risk of being an indicator occurrence. Indicator validity is the degree to which indicators identify events that merit further review.

8.   Development of an indicator-specific information set enhances the utility of the indicator.

Chapter 4 Study Questions

1. What is one solution for assessing outcomes of disaster preparedness when an outcome is difficult to measure?

2. Determine whether the following indicators are rate based (R) *or* continuous variable (C) *or* sentinel event (S); outcome (O) *or* process (P); and desirable (D) *or* undesirable (U):

    a. "Floodplain residents with flood insurance."

    R, C or S   O or P   D or U

    b. "Emergency-operations center warning lead time."

    R, C or S   O or P   D or U

c. "Pounds of obsolete locally-stockpiled medical therapeutics."

R, C or S   O or P   D or U

d. "Cycle time for dissemination of public disaster performance data."

R, C or S   O or P   D or U

e. "Hazard warning lead time, subcategorized by type of hazard."

R, C or S   O or P   D or U

f. "Firefighters certified as paramedics."

R, C or S   O or P   D or U

3. Determine which performance dimensions are measured by the indicators in #2 (e.g., efficiency, appropriateness). Recall that a single indicator may measure more than one dimension of performance.

4. Develop an indicator information set using the indicator development form for the indicators in question #2 or an indicator of your choosing.

Chapter 4 References

1. U.S. Department of Justice:
see http://www.usdoj.gov/ag/annual/reports/pr2001/Section01.htm.

2. U.S. Environmental Protection Agency:
see http:///www.epa.gov/safewater/pws/pn/handbook.pdf.

3. Rapid Assessment of Vectorborne Diseases During the Midwest Flood—United States, 1993. *MMWR*; July 8, 1994; 43(26); 481-3.

4. *Logistics Quarterly* 7, no. 2 (Summer 2001) see
http://www.lq.ca/summer2001/articles/article03.html.

5

Indicator Development Process

How are indicators developed? What are the development tasks to be performed and how is the work process best organized? What issues might arise during the development process? The answers to these questions constitute the essential components of the indicator development process.

Organizing the Indicator Development Process

Indicators are developed with the expectation that the information they generate will be used to improve the performance of processes and help achieve desired outcomes. Responsibility for the indicator development process begins with community governance and managers who must initiate and sustain their commitment to the process. Lacking leadership's commitment, the opportunity for continuously improving disaster-preparedness performance may fall short in spite of well-intentioned efforts by citizens, providers, and organizations.

The first step in a community-wide indicator development process is to convene a group of organization leaders and additional resource individuals. The members of this steering group should possess the values, knowledge, skills, attitudes, commitment, authority, and vision necessary to promote improvement in the core processes that comprise disaster preparedness. These leaders may benefit from external education, consultation, and technical assistance in performance-management and performance-measurement work methods. The group should clarify responsibilities for coordination of indicator development activities through the community; support these activities through allocation of sufficient resources; provide for education, consultation, and technical assistance in indicator work methods; and provide oversight for the indicator development effort.

The indicator development process generally relies on a group of selected experts to formulate a set of indicators with a reasonable degree of face validity. This approach is usually necessary for three reasons.

First, despite the vast amount of disaster literature, studies that address performance, particularly performance of an everyday nature, are rare. Thus, there is a paucity of reliable and valid information related to performance, and where studies on the same subject may be reported, widely variable results are common. Further, the development and application of large-scale databases are relatively recent phenomena and require sophisticated techniques and information-management experts. Expert consensus may lack scientific rigor, but its work products are likely to enjoy credibility at the onset.

Second, the expert consensus process has the advantage of fostering participant acceptance and support of indicator use. The desirability of involving and educating the providers who will actually use the performance indicators cannot be overemphasized. Without early acceptance, difficulties can be expected later, when providers are asked to evaluate indicator data, perform peer and systems' reviews, and recommend constructive actions.

Third, experts can contribute important knowledge about the community. This includes, for example, information about current and past programs, services offered by the community, and important linkages among the community's organizations, such as police and fire departments, emergency management agencies, hospitals, and public health agencies.

Two types of experts are required for the indicator development process—methodology experts and content experts. Methodology experts are individuals who have knowledge and experience in indicator development methods and who usually are also responsible for organizing and facilitating the development process. Content experts are individuals who have knowledge and experience pertinent to a specified core competence, i.e., disaster preparedness.

Both types of experts play a critical and complementary role in the development process. Content experts require a methodological framework that can capitalize on their contributions, and methodological experts require the substance to fill in the framework. The development process is characterized by a continual exchange of ideas and information between methodology and content experts. By the end of the development process, content and methodology experts should share a common body of knowledge relating to a specified core process (e.g., hazard analysis).

The indicator development process should be organized to make efficient use of community and expert resources. A useful approach to accomplish this goal is to divide the development process into two work phases. The first phase involves a subset of the full group of experts, including the methodology experts and selected content experts. Because organizations and their needs are unique, the specific identity of the methodology experts and content experts may vary. In certain instances, the community may choose to meet these needs through external consultation.

The second phase is characterized by expansion of the subgroup to include additional content experts. The addition of other content experts provides for broadened perspectives on important issues and permits early involvement and education of a larger number of the providers who will be using the indicators. In small organizations, it may be practical to consolidate the two work phases.

Development Process—Phase One

The subgroup's work plan consists of six tasks. These tasks constitute a considerable amount of work and are frequently delegated to individual staff members for execution between subgroup meetings. The six tasks are the following:

a. Selecting the group leader

b. Developing the charge to the full group

c. Delineating the core processes and outcomes that characterize a core competence

d. Developing a preliminary set of indicators

e. Developing indicator information sets

f. Selecting additional content experts to serve in the full group

Selecting the Group Leader

The subgroup, and later the full group, is led by a chairperson. The early identification and selection of a group leader creates an individual focus for integrating content and methodology expertise. The chairperson is usually a provider with demonstrated leadership qualities and appropriate training as well as considerable experience related to the area for which indicators are being developed.

Developing the Charge to the Full Group

The charge is the statement of purpose given to the full group. Drafted by subgroup members, it describes who the experts are, why they have been assembled, and what tasks they are going to perform.

Delineating the Core Processes and Outcomes That Characterize a Core Competence

Core processes and outcomes comprise each core competence. The core processes comprising disaster preparedness include, but are not limited to, hazard analysis, surveillance, warning, rehearsal, and logistics. Definition of core processes and outcomes by the subgroup should be preliminary, subject to further consideration by the full group.

Developing a Preliminary Set of Indicators

The content experts of the subgroup play the central role in this task. The preliminary set of indicators is an informed draft to which the full group can react with improvement suggestions, as appropriate. At least one indicator should be developed for each core process identified in step 3. The preliminary set of indicators developed by the subgroup is intended to stimulate, rather than constrain, the full group. It provides examples of indicators for those who are just becoming acquainted with the use of indicators as tools to measure performance. During full group meetings, content experts may accept a certain number of indicators as they are, refine or delete others, and create still more.

Developing Indicator Information Sets

An indicator information set should be developed for each preliminary indicator. (See Chapter 4.) This subgroup task is intended to educate full group members about the process of developing an information set so that their time is more efficiently used during the indicator development process.

Selecting Additional Content Experts to Serve in the Full Group

Determining the desired composition of the group is the first priority when selecting additional content experts to serve on the full group. The choice of professional groups that will be a part of the full group should be based on the constituencies involved in disaster preparedness. This process may be challenging, because many groups have an interest in disasters and more professional groups may want representation than is feasible. Full group members should be encouraged to review group composition at the first meeting and to add members as necessary.

Each group should include an information-management specialist. This individual provides knowledge and experience that will be helpful to content experts in linking proposed indicators to existing data. He or she will be able to provide important insights concerning data collectibility and reliability issues.

Development Process—Phase Two

Once the subgroup has completed its task, its work products should be distributed to full group members prior to the first meeting. Adequate meeting time must be provided to permit the full group to accomplish its objectives.

There are five major full group tasks:

1. Reviewing and revising the core processes of disaster preparedness

2. Reviewing group composition

3. Reviewing, revising, and finalizing the set of indicators

4. Defining data elements for each indicator

5. Identifying underlying factors that may explain variation in performance data

Reviewing and Revising the Core Processes of Disaster Preparedness

The preliminary set of core processes should be reviewed, revised, and refined as necessary. Where sound information underlies the identification of core processes, they may require few, if any, modifications. If there is an *a priori* expectation by subgroup members that major issues may arise, specific questions should be pre-identified to facilitate efficient discussion and resolution of the issues.

Reviewing Group Composition

Completing the previous task provides a basis for reevaluating the group membership. The need for additional content experts may become apparent as core competencies acquire clear dimensions.

Reviewing, revising, and finalizing the set of indicators

The development, refinement, and finalization of a set of indicators represent the key work of the full group. The list of preliminary indicators serves as the initial substrate for this activity. Indicators commonly undergo numerous refinements during this phase of indicator development.

Defining Data Elements for Each Indicator

Clear definitions of all data elements for each indicator are essential to ensure that the data elements can be collected in the form defined by the group. A data element is a single piece of data required by an indicator, subsequently aggregated in a manner with other data elements (that is, indicator data collection logic) to identify indicator event occurrences.

Identifying Underlying Factors That May Explain Variation in Performance Data

Content experts are essential in compiling a comprehensive list of underlying factors (that is, private citizen, providers, organization, community, state, and federal factors) that may explain variation in indicator data.

Indicator Development Process Issues

The indicator development process generally tends to flow smoothly. However, certain recurrent issues may be identified.

First, the literature on community disaster-preparedness performance, including data comparing performance among organizations (e.g., hospitals, public health agencies, emergency management agencies, police departments, and fire departments) and performance of an everyday nature, is extremely sparse. Groups and individuals that pursue expensive, time-consuming literature searches and reviews often come up relatively empty-handed simply because everyday performance has not been well-studied in the past. Where studies on the same subject do actually exist, widely varied results are common, leading to more dilemmas when deciding which researchers and/or data to accept. Considerable statistical expertise is often required to determine the validity of methodologies used to obtain the study results.

Many indicator development groups that have experienced an unsatisfying literature search choose to convene a panel of experts to develop indicators through the process of expert consensus. (See above, this chapter.) Expert consensus as to what constitutes a valid indicator may lack scientific rigor, but its work products are likely to enjoy credibility, at least in the beginning stages of performance measurement efforts.

Second, turf issues may arise during the indicator development process. Certain attitudes may be expressed during group meetings that reflect the deep beliefs of particular disciplines or departments. This phenomenon finds its fullest expression in groups where more than one professional discipline is providing services for the same disaster-preparedness process. Turf battles often represent a common symptom of underlying organization and community problems.

When such issues surface, it is important to emphasize that the focus of performance measurement, and indeed of disaster preparedness, is the community and its citizens, not providers or their organizations. Further, there is often little or no objective evidence to support many of these deeply held disciplinary beliefs. The indicator-development process offers an opportunity to create measures that can provide that evidence. Group members frequently relish this prospect. However, as the development process matures, group members come to realize that data can be a great leveler and that performance differences are more likely to exist between communities than between organizations and disciplines within a community.

Third, group members need to gain an early appreciation of data element definitional precision and collectibility issues. Content experts may require basic education concerning the need to develop indicators involving data elements that are readily collectible. An indicator may be a valid measure of preparedness, but its data elements may lack definitional precision and/or may not be readily collectible from source documents. In this case, the reliability of the indicator may decrease because a portion of the necessary data is inaccurate or incomplete. Some communities and organizations find they need to allocate resources to ensure the accuracy, completeness, and availability of important documentation before they can begin to measure important disaster-preparedness processes and outcomes.

Group members usually respond readily to the need for precise and collectible data elements once they become aware of these issues. In fact, members often develop a keen appetite to learn more about the spectrum of data issues, especially the issues that relate to the measurement of performance. The information-management specialist member of the group becomes a key figure during this process.

Fourth, indicator parsimony is a necessary precondition for data parsimony. Because of their enthusiasm, content members may initially propose a large number of indicators. Under such circumstances, reality testing is essential. Group members should be asked about their ability to manage the resulting data. Most communities have had, at best, limited experience managing and using performance data. A modest beginning is, in this instance, more likely to lead to an effective process. Ultimately, communities must be master of, and not slaves to, the data. They should collect only the data that is needed and use all the data that they have collected.

Fifth, there is a tendency to equate indicator data with actual level of performance. Group members need to be reminded that indicators and the data they generate are not direct measures of performance. Rather, indicators are tools used to direct attention to performance issues that might require more intense review within a community. Further investigation provides the basis for judgments regarding and approaches to performance-improvement opportunities.

Chapter 5 Summary Points

1. The indicator-development process requires the sustained commitment of community leadership.

2. In large communities, the development process may be divided into two phases to make more efficient and effective use of expert resources.

3. There are two kinds of experts who play complementary roles in the indicator-development process. Methodology experts have knowledge and experience in indicator-development methodology and are usually responsible for organizing and facilitating the development process. Content experts have knowledge and experience about the area for which indicators will be developed.

4. Indicator parsimony is a necessary precondition for data parsimony.

Chapter 5 Study Questions

1. List those whom you might select to be members of the subgroup for disaster-preparedness indicator development in your community.

2. Develop a preliminary list of core processes relating to disaster preparedness for your community.

3. Identify one performance indicator for each process in your list.

4. Based on items 2 and 3, who would you, as chairperson of the disaster-preparedness indicator development group, choose as representatives to serve in the *full group*?

6

Reliability and Validity: The Indicator Testing Process

In the past, indicators have been implemented before assessing and improving, when needed, their degrees of reliability and validity. When indicators possess high degrees of reliability and validity, the data and information they generate is more useful in continuously improving performance. Conversely, indicators that are unreliable and invalid produce confusing, irrelevant, and useless data and information while consuming precious resources. The testing process described in this chapter provides the opportunity to improve indicators' reliability and validity prior to their formal implementation.

Approach to Indicator Reliability and Validity Assessment

The reliability and validity of individual indicators need to be evaluated through systematic processes. These processes involve quantifying certain rates (for example, missing data element rates), determining why these rates exist, and then, to the extent possible, remedying the problems leading to the unacceptable degrees of reliability and/or validity.

The indicator reliability assessment process is distinct from validity testing. Nevertheless, the two processes are interlinked, because the degree to which an indicator is valid depends, in part, on the degree to which it reliably identifies the event that has been targeted for monitoring.

Indicator reliability measurement is the process of quantifying the completeness and accuracy with which indicator occurrences are identified from among all cases at risk of being indicator occurrences. An indicator's reliability is directly related to the quality of retrievable data. Data must be reasonably complete (that is, there must be a relatively low rate of missing data elements) and reasonably accurate (that is, there must be a relatively low rate of data errors) for an indicator to reliably identify the event of interest.

The final set of indicators that emerges from the development process described in Chapter 5 constitutes the focus of the testing phase. During this phase, the indicators are used for a period of time to determine the degree to which essential data is missing or inaccurate. For example, are essential data elements missing from source documents? Is essential data present in source documents but unavailable for abstraction purposes? Is the community adequately staffed to perform data collection and abstraction? Are abstractors adequately trained for use of the abstraction instrument? Is the abstraction instrument adequate?

When a cause of data incompleteness and/or inaccuracy is identified, it needs to be remedied, if possible. For example, if an indicator requires consistent documentation of whether a specified procedure was performed or not, improvement in the charting instrument (for example, development of a spreadsheet for documentation of hazards surveillance) often results in a reduced rate of missing data elements.

Data accuracy and missing data issues may arise with the introduction of a new measurement instrument. People who are experienced with indicator reliability issues stress to new users the following: 1) pre-testing abstraction instruments is helpful for early elimination of certain sources of error, 2) use of a computer as the abstraction instrument (as compared with manual abstraction) provides entry guidance through screen display, as well as powerful edit and range checks reduce the possibility of entry error, and 3) adequate attention to data element definitional precision, availability, and other data reliability issues must be a priority of content and methodology experts working together during the indicator-development phase. (See Chapter 5.)

In certain instances, it may not be possible to eliminate all data element collection problems. When this situation occurs, the effect of errors and missing data may be quantified and statistical confidence limits placed on the data when these rates are relatively low. For example, if a community's reported rate for an indicator is 45%, and it is known that unremedied errors can cause a +/- 5% rate distortion, then the community's actual rate is 45% +/-5%, or 40%–50%. If, however, the error rate for an indicator is relatively high (for example, 45%), the indicator rate may not be useful in measuring performance. The +/- rate distortion of an indicator rate of 45% includes 0% and is too large for users to have confidence in the results.

Indicator validity measurement is the process of quantifying the extent to which indicators identify events that merit further review. A reliable indicator can produce complete and accurate—but meaningless—data if, upon further review, the occurrences reliably identified by the indicator do not merit further review (that is, no opportunity to improve the process or outcome exists).

For sentinel event indicators, validity can be determined by quantifying the amount of agreement between occurrences identified by the indicators and occurrences that are then deemed to warrant further review. For a 100%-valid sentinel event indicator, each case identified will warrant further review. Sentinel event indicators that demonstrate an acceptable degree of concordance between those occurrences identified and those meriting further review may be judged valid.

Rate-based indicator validity testing involves a more complex approach because, by definition, a proportion of the occurrences identified by the indicator will *not* merit further review. The important assumption behind rate-based indicators is that higher-than-expected occurrence rates (or lower-than-expected occurrence rates, depending on an indicator's rationale), in theory, should reflect a greater proportion of occurrences that merit review.

To assess the validity of rate-based indicators, three determinations must be made. First, the rates should be composed substantially of true positive cases (that is, flagged cases in which the event of interest merits further review). Second, when rates vary over time, they do so primarily as a function of true positive occurrences needing review. Third, the differences in observed rates should be predominantly due to differences in the proportion of true positive occurrences meriting review.

When validity assessment for rate-based indicators is conducted, indicator occurrences (or a sampling thereof) need to be assessed to determine whether specific, objective, and predetermined reasons exist for excepting them from further review. Such reasons for exclusion are factors that are not amenable to improvement by the community and fully explain the occurrence; consequently, further review is not merited. This point bears emphasis. When exclusionary reasons have not been carefully delineated prior to review, determinations as to whether the case merits further review often become subjective, leading to results that may vary significantly among individuals, places, and times. When occurrences cannot be excepted based on the predetermined exclusionary reasons, they may be judged to merit further review.

When an indicator's degree of validity is unacceptable, processes need to be conducted to ascertain why, followed by modification of the indicator to resolve identified deficiencies. For example, consider that in one community, only 2% of identified (flagged) cases are valid occurrences (that is, warrant further review) for some rate-based indicator. This low yield of valid cases for the indicator needs to trigger a search for ways to improve the indicator. If improvement cannot be made, such an indicator may have to be eliminated, because it is not useful in its current form.

There are three reasons why an indicator's degree of validity may be unacceptable. First, *indicator reliability issues* may seriously affect an indicator's degree of validity. Inaccurate or missing data may result in a substantial number of cases that are misidentified (that is, false positives) or not identified at all (that is, false negatives). When false positive cases occur, the ensuing investigation often leads to frustration and wasted resources, because the event that the indicator is measuring does not exist in the incorrectly flagged cases. In the latter situation, an opportunity to improve a process may be lost because the indicator has failed to identify a case in which an event of interest actually does exist.

Second, *private-citizen, state, and federal factors* unrelated to community performance may affect an indicator's degree of validity. In this instance, a number of cases may be identified by the indicator, for which private-citizen, state, and federal factors clearly explain why the event occurred. No performance improvement opportunities related to community performance exist. For example, private citizens' expectations of "riding out the storm" (i.e., hurricane) may result in a relatively high average time for a hurricane time-to-evacuation indicator. In these instances, the opportunity for the community to improve the evacuation process and hurricane outcome may be limited.

Third, *an indicator may lack sufficient precision to eliminate certain cases from unnecessary further review or, alternatively, exceptions to the indicator may not have been developed and applied.* The ideal indicator is designed to exclude inappropriate cases from the review process. However, this may result in an indicator that itself becomes more cumbersome and confusing. For example, consider the indicator "time-to-evacuation following hurricane warning to evacuate, except for private citizens who, having been so notified, refuse to evacuate."

An alternative approach is to develop exceptions to the indicator that permit achievement of the same objective. Such exceptions (such as private citizens who, having been so notified, refuse to evacuate) may, for example, be applied to computer software and the database as edits designed to resolve identified imprecision in certain indicators. The validity of the indicator is thus retained.

Certain indicator deficiencies that lead to unacceptable validity may be resolved. First, problems with an indicator's reliability must be thoroughly addressed during the reliability assessment process, as previously discussed. In some instances, however, it may be necessary to eliminate an entire indicator because of one or more problematic data elements.

Second, for certain indicators, it may be possible to identify private-citizen factors that can be used to eliminate any significant variations that are due solely to one or more private citizen-specific factors and not to community performance. This may be accomplished, for example, by integrating such private-citizen factors directly into the indicator statement or by developing and integrating private-citizen-based exceptions to the indicator via edit during the abstraction process.

Chapter 6 Summary Points

1. A testing period for indicators is important because improving the degree of indicators' reliability and validity prior to their formal implementation will enhance their usefulness to communities.

2. Indicator reliability and validity assessments are distinct, but interlinked, processes.

3. Indicator reliability assessment is the process of quantifying the completeness and accuracy with which indicator occurrences are identified from among all cases at risk of being indicator occurrences.

4. Indicator validity assessment is the process of quantifying the extent to which indicators identify events that merit further review.

5. Validity assessments are more complex for rate-based indicators than for sentinel event indicators.

Chapter 6 Study Questions

1. As the rate of missing data elements decreases, the reliability of an indicator decreases. True or false?

2. An indicator may have a high degree of reliability but a low degree of validity. True or false?

3. An indicator may have a high degree of validity but a low degree of reliability. True or false?

4. Why is it important to have predetermined exclusionary reasons for why a case flagged by an indicator may be excepted from further review?

7

Summarizing Indicator Data

There comes a time when collected raw data needs to be sorted and organized, or summarized, in a form that enables users to make sense of it. Identifying important relationships from a mass of unsorted data is virtually impossible.

Summarizing data is the process of expressing unsorted raw data in a form that will permit, directly or by means of further calculations, conclusions to be drawn. Specifically, it involves developing frequency distributions and calculating for these distributions measures of central tendency and data spread. Measures of central tendency and spread allow for comparisons between frequency distributions, a topic addressed in Chapter 8. Differences between two distributions lead interpreters to seek reasons, or underlying factors, to explain the differences.

Indicator Data Frequency Distributions

A *frequency* is the number of times something occurs within a period of time. A *frequency distribution* (or, simply, distribution) is the complete summary of the frequencies of the values or categories of measurement made on a group of entities.

For example, consider the continuous data indicator "tornado warning lead time." Tornado warning lead time is the difference between the time a tornado warning is issued and the time the tornado affects the warned area. Table 7.1 lists the average number of minutes for tornado warning lead time for each year between 1992 and 2002, inclusive, e.g., 1992 = 7 minutes, 1993 = 6 minutes,…2002 = 12 minutes.

Table 7.1
Tornado Warning Lead Time (Annual Average, in Minutes)
1992–2002 [1-2]

Year	Average Minutes
1992	7
1993	6
1994	8
1995	10
1996	10
1997	9
1998	11
1999	12
2000	10
2001	10
2002	12

What is the frequency of the values 6, 7, 8, 9, 10, 11, and 12 minutes in this set of data? We can see the frequency distribution of this group of data in Figure 7.1.

Figure 7.1
Frequency Distribution for Tornado Warning Lead Time (Annual Average, in Minutes) 1992–2002

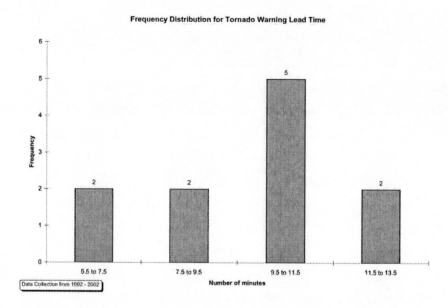

A bell-shaped curve, or normal distribution, is a familiar example of a distribution in which the greatest number of observations falls in the center with fewer and fewer observations falling evenly on either side of the average. We can see that Figure 7.1 is not a perfect bell-shaped curve; rather, it is slightly skewed to the right.

Important Characteristics of Distributions of Indicator Data

Once the raw observation data has been put into a frequency distribution, certain important values can be developed that describe the distribution's character. These values—measures of central tendency and spread—enable data interpreters to make comparisons between one set of data and another.

For example, consider the hypothetical data for tornado warning lead time for 1972 through 1982, inclusive. (See Table 7.2.)

Table 7.2
Tornado Warning Lead Time (Annual Average, in Minutes) 1972–1982

Year	Average Minutes
1972	2
1973	5
1974	3
1975	5
1976	6
1977	3
1978	8
1979	7
1980	6
1981	7
1982	6

The frequency distribution for the Table 7.2 data set is depicted in Figure 7.2:

Figure 7.2
Tornado Warning Lead Time (Annual Average, in Minutes)
1972–1982

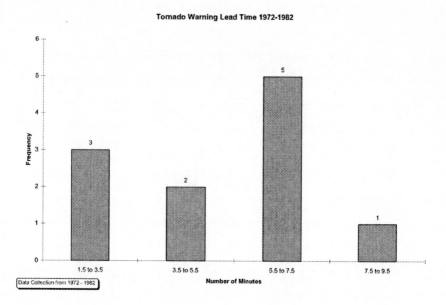

We can see that this frequency distribution does not conform to a normal, bell-shaped curve. We can see that Figures 7.1 and 7.2 are different from one another. This observed variability leads interpreters to ask why and to seek out underlying factors that may explain the variability. Buy how can we further describe the variability that we see between the two frequency distributions?

Measures of Central Tendency

We can further describe the variability between two frequencies by comparing measures of central tendency, e.g., between the data in Figures 7.1 and 7.2. The median, mean, and mode are three measures of central tendency for a given data set's frequency distribution. (See Table 7.3.)

Table 7.3
Definitions of Measures of Central Tendency

Measure of Central Tendency	Definition
Median	The middle value of a set of data
Mean	The average value of a set of data
Mode	The most common value of a set of data

Median

The median of a data set's frequency distribution is the middle number when the measurements are arranged sequentially from smallest to largest or from largest to smallest. *The median is the most valid measure of central tendency whenever a distribution is skewed.* The distributions in both Figures 7.1 and 7.2 are right-skewed.

Mean

The mean of a data set's distribution specifies the data set's arithmetic average—that is, the sum of all the measurements divided by the total number of measurements in the data set. The means for the tornado warning lead times in the 1972–1982 and 1992–2002 sets of measurements are 5.3 minutes and 9.6 minutes, respectively.

The mean is best used as a measure of central tendency when the distribution of data is balanced and when data are evenly distributed around a single value, as in a normal, bell-shaped curve. The mean may be affected by large outlying measurements, such as in skewed or asymmetric distributions. A median will be relatively unaffected by outlying measurements.

Mode

The mode of a data set's distribution is the value that occurs most often. In normally distributed data, the mean, median, and mode are identical. When the mean is greater than the median, the distribution will be right-skewed. When the mean is less than the median, the distribution will be left-skewed.

Figure 7.3
Relationship of the Mean, Median, and Mode to a Frequency Distribution's Skew

A. Normal Distribution: Mean = Median = Mode

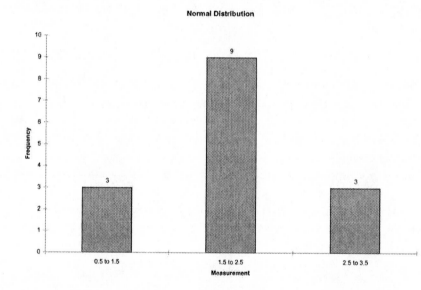

B. Right-Skewed Distribution: Mean > Median > Mode

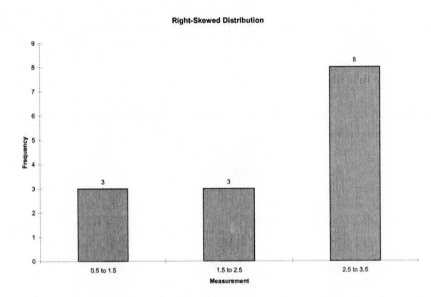

C. Left-Skewed Distribution: Mean < Median < Mode

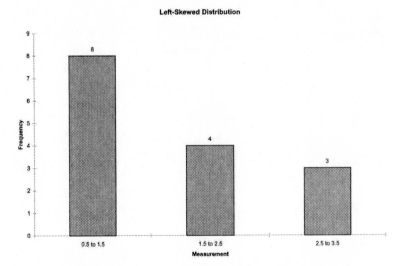

Measures of Dispersion

By itself, the data set's central location provides no information about data dispersion (also called spread, scatter, or variability). For example, consider the indicator "flash flood warning accuracy (in percent)." Accuracy is measured by the percent of times a flash flood actually occurs in an area that is covered by a flash flood warning.

Consider that the U.S.'s mean indicator rate for flash flood warning accuracy is 85%, meaning that 85% of the time, a flash flood actually occurs in an area that is covered by a flash flood warning. Also consider that 89% accuracy is the expressed "target" rate for predicting flash floods. Without knowledge of the data set's dispersion, one might conclude that all of the fifty states in the U.S. performed well in flash flood prediction accuracy.

However, we cannot presume that all of the states performed well in flash flood prediction accuracy until we know something about the data set's distribution. For example, consider the hypothetical situation that the states' percent accuracy ranged between 50% and 100%, with a mean calculating to 85%. The data suddenly become more interesting. Opportunities to improve the prediction process may be abundant among the states whose rates are dispersed far (downward) from the group's mean. For example, if one state's accuracy rate for predicting flash floods is only 50%, why? Without an idea of the data set's spread outward from the central measure, we could not ask this question and we would miss an opportunity to improve.

Three important measures of a data set's dispersion are the range, the standard deviation, and the interquartile range. (See Table 7.4.) The *range* is the distance between the lowest and highest values in a data set. It is calculated by subtracting the lowest value in the data set from the highest value in that same set. Its usefulness as a measure of dispersion is somewhat limited, because it is based on only the two extreme values in a data set and ignores the distribution of all the values within those limits.

Table 7.4
Definitions of Measures of Dispersion

Measure of Dispersion	Definition
Range	The difference between the lowest and highest values in a set of data
Standard deviation	Dispersion around the mean of a distribution; the square root of the variance
Interquartile range	Dispersion around the median of a distribution

For example, consider that the range for hazardous materials calls received by a communications center in 2001 is between 2 and 40 (range = 38). Then look at Figure 7.4 (below). The range does not provide the interesting information revealed by this graph, i.e., the spike in calls following the anthrax disaster in September and October 2001. The variability of the distribution is flat most of the time and then stacked up in a short period of time.

Figure 7.4
Calls received by the Idaho State Communications Center, August 1, 2001, to December 31, 2001 [3]

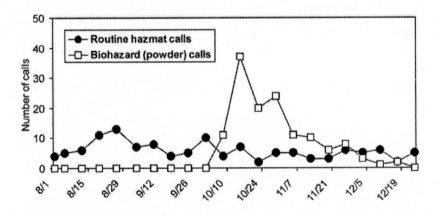

Standard deviation is another measure of variability that indicates the dispersion, spread, or variation in a distribution. It is equal to the square root of the mean of all the squares of the deviations from the mean.

For example, consider the indicator "population served by community water supplies receiving drinking water with no violations of any acute or chronic maximum contaminant level, acute or chronic treatment technique, or issuance of a health advisory." [4] The Environmental Protection Agency is the lead agency for primary enforcement authority and oversight of community water supply programs. The state of Illinois' EPA is working to increase the percent of its population served by clean water that doesn't make people sick. Its data set contains eight indicator rates for the years 1995–2002:

Table 7.5
Illinois Population Served Water without Violations

Year	Percent of Population
1995	88.96
1996	89.38
1997	92.75
1998	92
1999	91.47
2000	93.14
2001	93.28
2002	93.04

The arithmetic mean of this data set calculates to 91.75%. The deviation from this mean of 91.75% is calculated for each of the eight measurements in Table 7.6.

Table 7.6
Calculation of the Deviation from the Mean

Year	Indicator Mean	Population with EPA-Certified Water	Deviation	Square of Deviation
1995	91.75	88.96	91.75–88.96=2.79	7.78
1996	91.75	89.38	91.75–89.38=2.37	5.62
1997	91.75	92.75	91.75–92.75=-1	1
1998	91.75	92	91.75–92=-.25	.06
1999	91.75	91.47	91.75–91.47=.28	.08
2000	91.75	93.14	91.75–93.14=-1.39	1.93
2001	91.75	93.28	91.75–93.28=-1.53	2.34
2002	91.75	93.04	91.75–93.04=-1.29	1.66

Then the squares are added and the sum is divided by 8 (the number of measurements in the data set):

$$\frac{7.78 + 5.62 + 1 + .06 + .08 + 1.93 + 2.34 + 1.66}{8} = 20.47/8 = 2.56$$

The quotient, 2.56, is called the *variance.* The standard deviation is the square root of the variance. The square root of 2.56 is 1.61, which is also the standard deviation for this data set.

A large standard deviation (SD) shows that the distribution of the collected data is widely spread out from the mean, while a small standard deviation shows that the data is closely concentrated about the mean. Small standard deviation means small variability among measurements in the data set. Large standard deviation means large variability among numbers in the data set. Is a SD of 1.61% for the Illinois water indicator a large or small amount of variability in the data set?

The standard deviation measures the variability of a distribution in a single number or statistic. We have calculated that the standard deviation for the Illinois drinking water indicator is 1.61. We can subtract this standard deviation (1.61) from the arithmetic mean of 91.75—that is, 91.75-1.61—to obtain

90.14, which is "one standard deviation below the mean" or "-1 SD." One standard deviation above 91.75 (91.75 + 1.61) = 93.36 or "+ 1 SD."

We can calculate -2 SD and + 2 SD, as well as -3 SD and +3 SD, for a data set. (See Table 7.7.)

Table 7.7
Standard Deviations 1, 2, 3 for Illinois Water Purity Indicator

Mean (in percent of Illinois population receiving EPA-certified clean water between 1995 and 2002)	91.75
-1, +1 SD of the mean	90.14, 93.36
-2, +2 SD of the mean	88.53, 94.97
-3, +3 SD of the mean	86.92, 96.58

What do these measurements tell us? They tell us that, *in a normal distribution,*

- 68% of all measurements in the data set will fall between 90.14% and 93.36%,

- 95% of all measurements in the data set will fall between 88.53% and 94.97%, and

- 99.7% of all measurements in the data set will fall between 86.92% and 96.58%.

In addition to providing us with a useful measurement for summarizing the degree of variability in a particular data set, the standard deviation also enables us to determine whether the differences in variability observed between two distributions are more than likely to have arisen by chance alone (that is, is the difference significant?). We will discuss this further in Chapter 8.

The standard deviation tool has one major limitation. Standard deviations are useful in describing the range for curves that are normal distributions. But most data sets are *non-normal,* rather than normal, distributions. The standard deviation is meaningless in non-normally distributed data, because the proportions of values that fall within one or two or three standard deviations of the mean are not reasonably close to those predicted by the normal curve. Indeed, the pictorial of the Illinois water data (1995–2002) looks like the graph in Figure 7.5.

Figure 7.5
Illinois Population Served Water without Violations

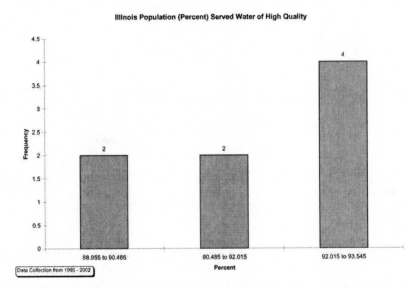

Does this look like a normal bell-shaped distribution? No. It is skewed to the right, meaning that its mean is greater than its median. *When data are not normally distributed, the most meaningful measure of dispersion is the interquartile range.*

Any distribution can be divided into equal, ordered subgroups called quantiles. Centiles, deciles, quintiles, and terciles are quantiles for distributions divided into hundredths, tenths, fifths, and thirds, respectively.

Four quartiles divide a distribution into four equal parts. A quartile's boundary is at the 25th, 50th, or 75th percentiles of such a distribution. The first quartile (Q1) is the point below which 25% of the values in the data set lie. The second quartile (Q2) falls at the distribution's median. Recall that the median is the middle value of a set of data (See Table 7.3.) The third quartile (Q3) is the point below which 75% of the values lie.

Interquartile range is a measure of dispersion around the median of a distribution. To calculate interquartile range, all values in the data set must first be arranged in increasing (or decreasing) order. Then the distribution is divided into equal subgroups, meaning that 25% of the values will lie between the minimum value and Q1, 25% of the values between Q1 and Q2, 25% of the values between Q2 and Q3, and 25% of the values between Q3 and the maximum value of the data set. The interquartile range is the range in values between Q1 (25% of the observations) and Q3 (75% of the observations).

Figure 7.6
Interquartile Range: A Measure of Dispersion around a Distribution's Median

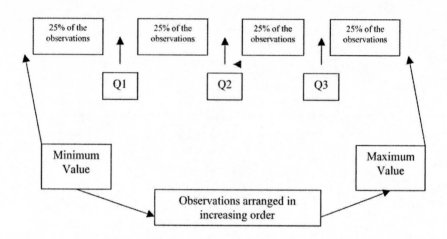

Consider once again the Illinois water indicator (See Figure 7.7.) The median for this indicator is 92.375. Half of the values in our data set are equal to or larger than the median and half have values are equal to or smaller than the median.

Figure 7.7
Interquartile Range for Data on Illinois Population Served Water without Violations

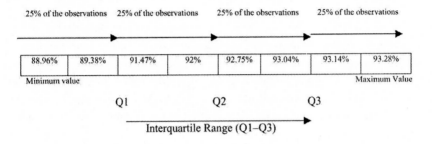

The interquartile range is the range in values between Q1 (90.425%) and Q3 (93.09%), which calculates to 2.67%. Using the interquartile range measure of dispersion, we can say that from 1995–2002, between 90.425% and 93.425% of Illinois' population had EPA-certified pure water. The median and interquartile range are better suited for non-normal distributions, because they are less sensitive to outlying values.

Chapter 7 Summary Observations

1. Summarizing data is the process of expressing unsorted raw data in a form that will permit, either directly or by means of further calculations, conclusions to be drawn.

2. A frequency distribution, or, simply, distribution, is the complete summary of the frequencies of the values or categories of measurement made on a group of entities.

3. A bell-shaped curve, or normal distribution, is an example of a distribution in which the greatest number of observations (measurements) falls in the center, with fewer and fewer observations falling evenly on either side of the arithmetic average, or mean. Most data does not conform readily to a normal distribution. Rather, distributions are skewed to the left or to the right.

4. The median, mean, and mode are three measures of central tendency for a distribution.

5. The median of a data set's distribution is the middle number when the mea-surements are arranged sequentially from smallest to largest or from largest to smallest. It is the most valid measure of central tendency whenever a dis-tribution is skewed. It is often used in conjunction with the interquartile range.

6. The mean of a distribution specifies the arithmetic average—that is, the sum of all the measurements divided by the total number of measurements in the data set. The mean is best used as a measure of central tendency when the distribution of data is balanced, as in a normal curve, because the mean may be affected by large outlying measurements, such as in skewed, or asymmet-ric, distributions. The mean is often used in conjunction with the standard deviation.

7. Three measures of dispersion for a distribution are the range, the standard deviation, and the interquartile range.

8. The interquartile range is a measure of dispersion around the median of a distribution and is most useful in describing non-normally distributed data. The interquartile range is often used in conjunction with the median.

Chapter 7 Study Questions

1. Calculate the mean, median, and mode for the data in Table 7.8 on the num-ber of state and local bomb technicians trained by the Federal Bureau of Investi-gation [5]

Table 7.8: State and local bomb technicians trained

Year	Number of State and Local Bomb Technicians Trained
FY1997	384
FY1998	681
FY1999	1,415
FY2000	1,378
FY2001	861
FY2002	882

2. Does the frequency distribution for data in Table 7.8 approximate a normal or a non-normal frequency distribution? Why is this important information to know?

3. Calculate the standard deviation and the interquartile range for the data in Table 7.8.

4. Are most frequency distributions normal or non-normal in shape?

Chapter 7 References

1. Centers for Disease Control and Prevention:
see http://www.cdc.gov/ncidod/EID/vol8no10/02-0390-G.htm.

2. National Weather Service:
see http://tgsv5.nws.noaa.gov/ost/nws_sci_needs_final_02_20-02.pdf.

3. Centers for Disease Control and Prevention:
see http://www.cdc.gov/ncidod/EID/vol8no10/02-0390-G.htm.

4. U.S. Environmental Protection Agency:
see http://www.epa.gov/safewater/standard/leadfr.html.

5. U.S. Department of Justice:
see http://www.usdoj.gov/ag/annual_reports/pr2002/Section01.htm.

8

Variation in Data

Measurements of a system or process invariably fluctuate over time. The amount of variation in data is measured by its dispersion (e.g., standard deviation, inter-quartile range) around its central location (e.g., mean, median) in its unique frequency distribution, as discussed in Chapter 7. Unfortunately, knowing *how much* variability exists in a data set does not answer the question, "*When* should one take action on the variation in data one is observing?"

This question challenged the fertile mind of a young engineer named Walter A. Shewhart. In the 1920s, he worked at Western Electric Company, a manufacturer of telephone hardware for Bell Telephone in Chicago. He was assigned the problem of improving the reliability of Bell Telephone transmission systems. Because amplifiers and other equipment had to be buried underground, there was a business need to reduce the frequency of failures and repairs. Bell Telephone had already realized the importance of reducing variation in manufacturing processes.

Shewhart single-handedly created a vast system for understanding variation. It is based on three discoveries:

1) The idea of common causes and special causes

2) The idea that people often over- or under-react to variation.

3) The idea of the control chart to help users react appropriately to variation

In two slim volumes, Shewhart laid out the entire field of statistical quality control, including its theory, philosophy, applications, and economic aspects. Both books remain in publication today. They are: *Economic Control of Quality of Manufactured Product* (first published in 1931) and *Statistical Method from the Viewpoint of Quality Control* (first published in 1939).

The Idea of Common and Special Cause Variation

Shewhart posited two sources of variation: common cause and special cause. W. Edwards Deming, who discovered and popularized the work of Shewhart, said, "This in itself was a great contribution to knowledge." [1]

Common-cause variation is fluctuation in a series of data results that is due to the process itself and interactions of variables of that process. Common-cause variation is inherent in all processes. Individual common causes have a relatively minor effect, but taken together they contribute to increased variability in measurements. This variability occurs even when all conditions are held as constant as is humanly possible. Common causes *are* the system and can be removed only when the system or process undergoes fundamental re-engineering.

For example, consider the indicator "tornado warning lead time," which is defined as the difference between the time a tornado warning is issued and the time the tornado affects the warned area. As long as people use and read different timepieces (clocks, watches), a certain minimal amount of data fluctuation (seconds here, seconds there) will occur for this indicator. Common causes of variation remain the same from day to day, lot to lot. The only way to eliminate common causes from a process or system is to change the process or system. The new system, however, will have its own common causes that influence the results. The synonyms for common-cause variation include chance cause, random cause, endogenous cause, and systemic cause variation.

Special-cause variation is the fluctuation in a series of results that is due to factors that intermittently and unpredictably induce variation over and above that inherent in a particular system. Special causes of variation are not part of the system, but they arise because of specific circumstances outside of the system.

For example, consider the number of daily hazardous materials calls received by a communications center in 2001, previously discussed in Chapter 7. The dramatic spike in calls between 10/10 and 11/7 was caused by a special cause—that is, biohazard anthrax powder calls. (The wavy baseline that exists most of the time for this indicator is due to common causes.)

Figure 8.1

Calls received by the Idaho State Communications Center, August 1, 2001, to December 31, 2001 [2]

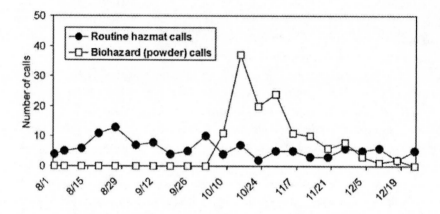

Several typical differences distinguish common and special causes of variation. Usually, common causes are large in number, the effect of each is slight, and, on an individual basis, they may not be worth seeking out. Usually, special causes are few in number (perhaps only one), the effect of each is marked, and they are well worth seeking out. In fact, they need to be investigated without delay. To remove common causes means to fundamentally change the process. This task belongs to managers. To remove a special cause means to fix the existing process. This task belongs to workers who are intimately involved with the process.

People's Over-Reaction or Under-Reaction to Variation

Shewhart's second discovery involved the two kinds of mistakes that people make in the process of reacting to variation. The first kind of mistake is to react to variation as if it came from a special cause when it actually came from common causes of variation. The second kind of mistake is to treat variation as if it came from common causes of variation when actually it came from a special cause. People who are prone to the first kind of mistake are over-reactors, and people who are prone to the second mistake are under-reactors.

Over-reactors believe that observed variation is the result of something exceptional, usually one obvious cause. This cause, once identified, is analyzed in excruciating detail and acted on with vigor. Over-reactors do not understand that variation is inherent in the output of every dynamic system and that every observed fluctuation in output does not necessarily warrant reaction or action.

Over-reactors are prone to *tampering*—that is, acting on variation without taking into account the difference between the two sources of variation: special cause and common cause. Deming illustrated tampering with his famous "funnel experiment," which demonstrates the losses that are caused by overreacting to variation. [3] Peter Senge describes tampering as a "fixation on events," which is one of seven learning disabilities that may afflict organizations. [4] *The net result of tampering is to throw the system farther and farther out of control, thereby increasing, rather than decreasing, variation.*

Under-reactors believe that variation is the result of failing to comply with standards and practices. As long as people do what the standards tell them to do, the reasoning goes, uniform results follow and variation ceases to exist. Worrying about variation, according to under-reactors, is a waste of time. They ignore the possibility. When a desired level of performance is not achieved, the recourse is to deal more stringently with standards noncompliance.

There are three problems with this approach. First, standards may be arbitrary or developed with insufficient information and knowledge of a system's capability to achieve prescribed results. Deming's famous "red bead experiment" illustrates this issue well. [5] In this experiment, "willing workers" can never meet the arbitrary goals (process specifications) set by the managers because the system in which they are asked to work is incapable of producing the output the managers expect. Bounds et al state, "Managing to arbitrary targets, rewarding or praising those who exceed them and penalizing or berating those who fail to meet them is founded in the theory that variation should not exist." [6]

Second, forcing people to work toward meeting unrealistic standards can actually hurt outcomes. People may concentrate on complying with known standards—that is, those for which people believe they will be graded. Other important dimensions of performance that are not being monitored may be neglected. Workers may be fully aware that their effort to improve a monitored dimension of performance is occurring at the expense of unmonitored dimensions.

Third, ignoring variation may lower workers' self-esteem. A worker who cannot meet expectations for process specifications, however unrealistic they may be, will not feel good. When workers become fearful and demoralized, the success of the organization becomes imperiled.

Introduction to Shewhart Control Charts

Shewhart's third discovery was a *control chart* for interpreting variation in data. Shewhart wrestled with the presence of random variation in data. He then realized that the problem was statistical in nature. Some of the observed variation in performance data was natural to the process and unavoidable. From time to time, however, variations in data would arise that could not be so explained. Shewhart concluded that statistical limits could be placed upon the natural variation of any process, so that fluctuations within these limits would be readily explained by common causes, but any variation outside the limits would indicate that something had fundamentally changed in the underlying process.

A *control chart* is a graphic display of data in the order that they occur, with statistically determined upper and lower limits of expected common-cause variation. [7] Shewhart devised the control chart to provide a consistent method to examine variation within processes over time and to link variation to its common cause or special cause sources. The control chart and its rules for use give interpreters an excellent means to make clear and repeatable judgments about statistical control of variation in results. The primary advantage of using a control chart is the ability to minimize the economic loss that comes from mistakes that occur when humans react inappropriately to variation.

Shewhart's discovery of control charts was a stunning advance upon *run charts,* which are displays of performance data in which data points are plotted as they occur over time to detect trends or other patterns in variation over time. [8] For example, Figure 8.2 is a simple run chart depicting the annual average (in minutes) for flash flood warning lead time.

Figure 8.2
Example of Run Chart: Flash Flood Warning Lead Times [9]

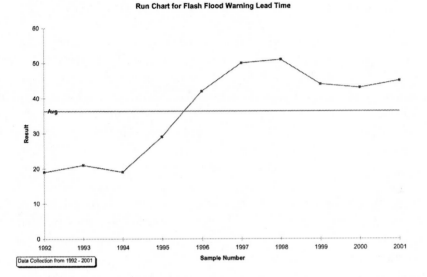

Does the run chart in Figure 8.2 show little variation or great stability? Can you determine from this run chart whether the variation in data points stems from common causes or special causes? Should you make or not make changes based on what you observe? These are important questions to most interpreters, because variation stemming from common causes ordinarily requires no immediate action, whereas variation stemming from special causes does. Yet, it is usually not possible to answer these questions from the information provided on the run charts.

Most people experienced in interpreting run charts agree about the frustration associated with figuring out the meaning of a high or low data point on a graph. Shewhart's approach guides the interpreter to ask whether a high or low point indicates the presence of a special cause, which requires action, or common causes, which require no immediate action. The way to ascertain the meaning of data points on a run chart is to rely on probability as a guide.

The basis of all control charts is that any varying quantity forms a frequency distribution if common causes alone are at work. Any such distribution will also have a mean and a standard deviation. Burr explains,

Quite regardless of the shape of the distribution (unless extremely badly behaved), there will be, *by chance causes only, very few points outside of the band between the central location (mean) minus three standard deviations (3 SD) and the mean plus three standard deviations.* Hence, having set such limits, we have a band of normal variability for the statistical measure in question. [10]

For example, consider that a data point for one time interval, say, one month, is due to a rare "ganging up" of common causes, and that no special cause is at work. It is still a much better bet that the point outside the band is due to some special cause. If a point comes along that is *outside* of the +3SD or -3SD limits, we assume that a special cause is indeed at work and try to see what process conditions might have changed and what needs fixing. Conversely, a point lying *inside* the control band does not evoke special causes; rather, it suggests that no reliable evidence exists for supposing that a special cause at work. Hence, no action is taken. Points within the band are attributed to common causes only.

For example, consider Figure 8.3, which is the run chart of Figure 8.2, to which center line and control limits have been added. The control limits are the boundaries for the upper and lower bands of normal variability. Now interpreters can readily ascertain which data points are in control and which show evidence of special causes. An upper control limit (UCL) is set at +3 SDs from the mean (highest hatched line) and a lower control limit (LCL) is set at -3SDs from the mean (lowest hatched line). Note the five data points on or beyond the UCL and LCL. We will return to these later.

Figure 8.3
Control Chart for Flash Flood Warning Lead Time

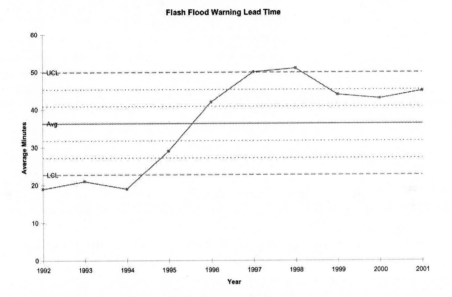

Flash Flood Warning Lead Time

Advantages of a Process in Good Control

There are at least five advantages to having a process brought into control. [11]

1. An in-control process can be assumed to be free from sources of variation that are worth identifying. The process as currently designed and executed is doing all that can be expected of it. To improve on the process' output requires fundamental change in the process itself (that is, removing common causes).

2. Getting a process into good statistical control ordinarily involves identifying and removing undesirable special causes or including some desirable special causes. For instance, Figure 8.4 shows five data points (1992, 1993, 1994, 1997, and 1998) that lie *outside* of 3 SDs of the mean. The flash flood warning time process is *not* in control. Special causes were operating in 1992, 1993, and 1994, when the lead time was shorter, and special causes were operating in 1997 and 1998, when the lead time surpassed the fifty-minute mark.

3. Any process that is in good control is predicable and stable. Variation is consistent, and the results fluctuate randomly around a steady average. Customers of the process know what to expect. An out-of-control process, by contrast, is unpredictable and unstable. Variation in an out-of-control process is inconsistent over time, shows a changing average, or shows no systematic pattern over time. Users of the process never know what to expect. For instance, a flood plain resident does not know whether a flash flood will arrive in eighteen minutes or fifty minutes or, if flash flood prediction accuracy is low (a separate indicator), whether the flash flood will arrive at all. Each time users receive output from an out-of-control process, such as a flash flood warning, they need to inspect the output to make a judgment about what exactly to do with the information. When a process is out of control in a statistical sense, special causes need to be identified.

4. When a process is in good control, the output is predictably known, so that assurances can be offered to users about the reliability of the process.

5. The best way to decrease the need for inspection is by bringing a process in control. Inspection involves measuring, examining, testing, or gauging one or more characteristics of an outcome and comparing these results with specified requirements to determine conformity. Inspection is a past-oriented strategy that attempts to identify unacceptable output after it has been produced and then separate it from the good output.

    Inspection is very expensive. Deming admonished people to cease depending on mass inspection [12]. He asserted, "Inspection with the aim of finding the bad ones and throwing them out is too late, ineffective, costly...In the first place, you can't find the bad ones, not all of them. Second, it costs too much. Quality comes not from inspection but from improving the process." [13]

Chapter 8 Summary Points

1. Measurements of a system or process invariably fluctuate over time.

2. Shewhart made three important discoveries about variation: (1) the idea of common causes and special causes, (2) the idea that people make the mistake of either reacting to variation as if it came from a special cause (when it actually came from common causes) or reacting to variation as if it came from common causes (when it actually came from one or more special causes), and

(3) the idea of the control chart to help users better interpret observed variation (know when to and when not to act on data variation).

3. Tampering is taking action on some signal of variation without considering the source of variation (common cause or special cause).

4. Common-cause variation is the fluctuation in a series of results that comes from the process itself. It is inherent in all processes and systems.

5. Special-cause variation is the fluctuation in a series of results that comes from factors intermittently and unpredictably above and beyond the variation inherent in a process or system. Special causes of variation are not part of the process or system all the time; rather they arise because of specific circumstances.

6. A control chart is a graphic display of data in the order that they occur with statistically determined upper and lower limits of expected common-cause variation. A control chart is used to identify special causes of variation, to monitor a process for maintenance, and to determine if process changes have had the desired effect. The primary advantage of using a control chart that it minimizes the economic loss that comes from mistakes that occur in interpreting the meaning of variation.

7. Data points lying outside the normal band of variability (beyond the control limits) on a control chart indicate that the process or outcomes is out of control, that special causes of variation are likely in play, and that action is required to identify the special causes.

Chapter 8 Study Questions

1. Analyze the following graphs for common cause and special-cause variation and opportunities to improve the process undergoing measurement:

a.

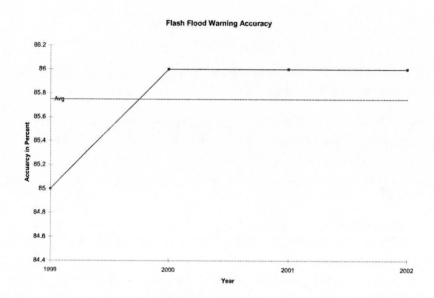

b.

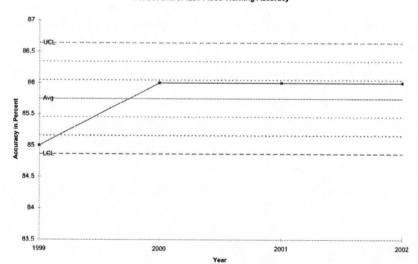

2. Evaluate Figure 8.3 for sources of variation. Are special causes of variation always undesirable? If yes, explain. If no, explain.

Chapter 8 References

1. W. E. Deming, *The New Economics for Industry, Government, Education* (Cambridge, MA: Massachusetts Institute of Technology Center for Advanced Engineering Study, 1993) 178.

2. See: http://www.cdc.gov/ncidod/EID/vol8no10/02-0390-G.htm.

3. Deming, *New Economics,* 194–209.

4. P. Senge, *The Fifth Discipline: The Art and Practice of the Learning Organization* (New York: Doubleday Currency, 1990) 21.

5. Deming, *New Economics,* 158–175.

6. G. Bounds, L. Yorks, M. Adams, et al, *Beyond Total Quality Management: Toward the Emerging Paradigm* (New York: McGraw-Hill, 1994) 353–354.

7. Joint Commission on Accreditation of Healthcare Organizations: *Lexikon* (Oakbrook Terrace, IL, 1994) 215.

8. Ibid, 703.

9. See: http://www.whitehouse. gov/omb/budget/fy2004/pma/nationalweather.pdf.

10. I. Burr, *Statistical Quality Control Methods* (New York: Marcel Dekker, 1976) 26–28.

11. Ibid, 23–34.

12. W. E. Deming, *Out of the Crisis* (Cambridge, MA: Massachusetts Institute of Technology, Center for Advanced Engineering Study, 1986.

13. M. Walton, *The Deming Management Method* (New York: Perigee Books, Putnam Publishing Group, 1986) 60.

9

Factors Influencing Variation

Understanding the causes of variation in performance data is the final task of the interpretive process. The causes of variation need to be laid out and prioritized in the order in which the causes need to be addressed. Synonyms of underlying causes of variation include factors, cause factors, underlying factors, root causes, reasons, underlying reasons, problems, and underlying problems.

Examining Variation Behavior for Performance Improvement Activities

The information contained in variation forms the basis for two broad categories of performance-improvement activities:

- Stabilizing an out-of-control process
- Improving an in-control process

Stabilizing an out-of-control process involves taking action on statistical signals of change (special causes) that are detected in results plotted on control charts. The object is to maintain a steady state—that is, a steady level of variation around a steady average. Once a statistical signal of change is detected in a control chart, the underlying special cause(s) need to be identified.

Improving an in-control process involves taking action on a process that is in good control but which does not meet users' needs or expectations. Good control does not necessarily mean that a given process is adequately meeting users' expectations or needs. It only means that the process is consistent; it may be consistently mediocre or even consistently bad.

Process performance is most commonly improved by changing the process average indicated by the center line of a control chart. This is clearly what is happening in Figure 9.1—that is, the process average is increasing (in this indicator, improving) over time.

Figure 9.1
Run Chart with Changing Average: Flash Flood Warning Lead Times

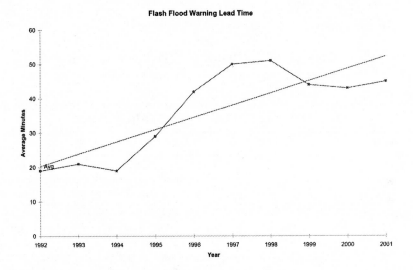

Tools and Methods to Identify Causes of In-Control and Out-of-Control Process Variation

A large number of tools and methods exist for finding causes of variation. Tools used for identifying special causes for out-of-control processes or common causes for in-control processes are the same. These tools and methods include

- Brainstorming
- Cause-and-effect diagrams
- Checksheets
- Control charts
- Flowcharts
- Force field analysis
- Histograms
- Nominal group techniques
- Pareto charts

- Process capability
- Run charts
- Scatter diagrams
- Stratification

Table 9.1 defines five of the techniques: flow charts, cause-and-effect diagrams, brainstorming, Pareto charts, and checksheets.

Table 9.1
Definition of Five Quality Control Techniques

Technique	Definition
Flowchart	Pictorial summary that shows with symbols and words the steps, sequence, and relationship of the various operations involved in performing a process
Cause-and-effect diagram	A tool used to analyze all factors (causes) that contribute to a given situation or occurrence (effect) by breaking down main causes into smaller and smaller sub-causes, also known as the Ishikawa or the "fishbone diagram"
Brainstorming	The process of eliciting large numbers of ideas from a group that is encouraged to use its collective thinking power to generate ideas and unrestrained thoughts in a relatively short period, often used to generate the underlying causes for a cause-and-effect diagram
Pareto chart	A special form of vertical bar graph that displays information in such a way that priorities for process improvements can be established, displays the relative importance of all the data and is used to direct efforts to the largest improvement opportunity by highlighting the vital few in contrast to the many others
Checksheet	A data-collection form that summarizes counts for individual cause categories; used to answer the question, "How often are certain events happening?" and is key to translating opinions into facts; used in constructing a Pareto diagram

These techniques for identifying underlying causes of variation can be very helpful when used appropriately. However, as Kaoru Ishikawa warns,

Too often, a tool for data analysis is used for its own sake, out of the context of systematically building knowledge and taking action for improvement. This may be done in the mistaken belief that the tool is able to lead the user to ask the right questions about the process. Unfortunately no tool is able to provide a rationale for analysis or a substitute for thought. [1]

Ishikawa also warns about the indiscriminate use of quality-control tools and techniques. He recalls that in the 1950s, the use of certain statistical tools and methods created a number of problems in Japan, including fear and dislike of quality control because workers did not understand the methods. "It is true that statistical methods are effective, but we overemphasized their importance. We overeducated people by giving them sophisticated methods where, at that stage, simple methods would have sufficed." [2]

Many good books have been published on the tools and methods for the improvement of quality once the decision to act on data has been made.[1-6] Nevertheless, experts in performance measurement contend that the best source of knowledge about underlying factors is the people who are closest to the process undergoing measurement—that is, the content experts.

Chapter 9 Summary Points

1. Understanding the causes of variation in a series of disaster-preparedness performance data is the final task of the interpretive process.

2. There are many tools available for finding causes of variation. Indiscriminate use of quality-control tools and techniques can cause problems.

3. The best source of knowledge about underlying factors to explain observed variation is the people who are closest to the process undergoing measurement, i.e., the content experts.

Chapter 9 Study Questions

1. Explain why users might want to identify underlying factors for a core process in disaster preparedness that is already in control.

2. List three community disaster-preparedness core processes that are out of control.

3. List three community disaster-preparedness core processes that are in control.

4.   What is the purpose(s) of having a process in control?

Chapter 9 References

1.   G. Bounds, L. Yorks, M. Adams, et al, *Beyond Total Quality Management: Toward the Emerging Paradigm* (New York: McGraw-Hill, 1994) 393.

2.   K. Ishikawa (David Lu, translator), *What Is Total Quality Control? The Japanese Way* (Englewood Cliffs, NJ: Prentice-Hall, 1985) 18–19.

3.   H. Gitlow, S. Gitlow, A. Oppenheim, et al, *Tools and Methods for the Improvement of Quality* (Homewood, IL: Irwin, 1989).

4.   M. Brassard, D. Ritter, *The Memory Jogger II*. Goal/QPC; 1st edition (January 15, 1994).

5.   R. W. Peach, M. Brassard, and D. Ritter, *The Creativity Tools Memory Jogger*. Goal/QPC; June 1998.

6.   R.C. Swanson, *The Quality Improvement Handbook: Team Guide to Tools and Techniques* (City: Saint Lucie Press, 1995).

Afterword

Measuring Disaster Preparedness started with the premise that the best way to improve a process is to measure it. *Measuring Disaster Preparedness* will have succeeded in its purpose if readers now better understand two things: 1) the power of scientific measurement to improve all the measures undertaken by communities in anticipation of imminent disaster, e.g., surveillance, warning, and rehearsals, and 2) the need to internalize measurement into community processes *now* to increase the probability that communities will rebound from the severe social stresses that increasingly characterize the world we inhabit.

Glossary

Aggregate data indicator A type of indicator, based on collection and aggregation of data about many events or phenomena. The events or phenomena may be desirable or undesirable, and the data may be reported as a continuous variable or a discrete variable. The two major types of aggregate data indicators are rate-based indicators (also called discrete variable indicators) and continuous variable indicators. *See also* continuous variable indicator; indicator; rate-based indicator; sentinel event indicator.

All-hazards approach A management approach that uses the same set of management arrangements to deal with all types of hazards (natural, manmade, complex). *See also* complex hazard; manmade hazard; natural hazard.

Appropriateness The degree to which the correct process is performed or the correct outcome is achieved, given the current state of knowledge; a dimension of performance. *See also* dimensions of performance.

Assessment The process of determining the value, significance, or extent of something, as in performance assessment. *See also* performance assessment; vulnerability assessment.

Assessment, performance *See* performance assessment.

Assessment, vulnerability *See* vulnerability assessment.

Assignable cause *See* special cause.

Assignable-cause variation *See* special-cause variation.

Availability The degree to which a process output is capable of being used, given the current state of knowledge; a dimension of performance. *See also* dimensions of performance.

Average *See* mean; measures of central tendency; median; mode.

Bell-shaped curve *See* frequency distribution.

Benchmark A point of reference or standard by which something can be measured or judged. The origins of the term benchmark derive from a mark made on a stationary object of previously determined position and elevation and used as a reference point in tidal observations and surveys. *See also* benchmarking.

Benchmarking To study someone else's processes and outcomes to learn how to improve one's own.

Brainstorming A process used to elicit a large number of ideas from a group of people who are encouraged to use their collective thinking power to generate ideas and unrestrained thoughts in a relatively short period of time.

Case-based review An approach to evaluating performance that involves addressing an issue using information and knowledge previously gained in a similar situation. *See also* standards-based review.

Cause-and-effect diagram A pictorial display drawn to represent the relationship between some "effect" and all the possible "causes" influencing it. *Synonyms*: fishbone diagram (because of its appearance); Ishikawa diagram (after the individual, Kaoru Ishikawa, who first developed and applied the tool).

Center line The line on a graph representing the average (for example, the mean, mode, or median). *See* control chart.

Certainty, hazard *See* hazard certainty.

Chart, run *See* run chart.

Checksheet A data-collection form that helps to summarize data based on sample observations and begins to identify patterns. A checksheet is used to answer the question, "How often are certain events happening?" It starts the process of translating "opinions" into "facts." The completed form displays the data in a simple graphic summary. *Synonym*: check sheet.

Chemical A good produced by or used in a reaction involving changes in atoms or molecules.

Chemical facility All buildings, structures and other stationary items that are located on a single site or a contiguous or adjacent site and which are owned or operated by the same person and which actually manufacture, produce, use, transfer, store, supply, or distribute any hazardous material. The term includes railroad yards and truck terminals but does not include individual trucks, rolling stock, water vessels, airplanes, or other transportation vehicles. *See also* chemical; hazardous material.

Common cause An ever-present factor that contributes to the random variation inherent in all processes. Common causes of variation are endogenous to a system and are not disturbances (they *are* the system) and can be removed or eliminated only by making basic changes to the system. *Synonyms:* endogenous cause; systemic cause. *Compare* special cause. *See also* common-cause variation; variation.

Common-cause variation Fluctuation in a process that is due to the process itself and is produced by interactions of variables of that process. Common-cause variation is inherent in all processes. *Synonyms:* endogenous-cause variation; systemic-cause variation. *Compare* special-cause variation. *See also* common cause; process variation; tampering; variation.

Community A relatively complex and relatively permanent geopolitical entity (an entire city, village, incorporated town, county, or parish) that has defined legal boundaries.

Complex disaster A state or condition destabilizing a social system caused by the action of natural *and* manmade forces. *See also* disaster; natural disaster; technological disaster.

Complex hazard An extreme phenomenon caused by the combined action of natural and manmade forces that has the potential to harm human settlements, e.g., a tornado striking a hazardous-materials storage site or a downed power line igniting a wildland fire during high winds. *See also* hazard; natural hazard; technological hazard.

Continuous quality improvement (CQI) *See* performance management.

Continuous Uninterrupted in time, sequence substance or extent, as in continuous improvement. *See also* continuous data.

Continuous data Data with a potentially infinite number of possible values along a continuum. *See also* continuous.

Continuous variable A variable that, when measured, has a potentially infinite number of possible values along a continuum. *Compare* discrete variable. *See also* continuous data; continuous variable indicator.

Continuous variable indicator An aggregate data indicator in which the value of each measurement can fall anywhere along a continuous scale. *Compare* rate-based indicator. *See also* aggregate data indicator; continuous variable; indicator.

Control 1) To exercise authority or influence over. 2) That aspect of management concerned with the comparison of actual versus planned performance. *See also* statistical control.

Control chart A graphic display of data in the order that they occur with statistically determined upper and lower limits of expected common-cause variation. A control chart is used to indicate special causes of variation, to monitor a process for maintenance, and to determine if process changes have had the desired effect. *See also* common-cause variation; run chart; special cause; special-cause variation; statistical control.

Control limit In statistics, an expected limit of common-cause variation, sometimes referred to as either an upper or a lower control limit. Variation beyond a control limit is evidence that special causes are affecting a process. Control limits are calculated from process data and are not to be confused with engineering specifications or tolerance limits. Control limits are typically plotted on a control chart. *See also* common-cause variation; control chart; special-cause variation; specification; statistical control.

Control, statistical *See* statistical control.

Coordination The degree to which a process is performed in congruent action across communities, organizations, providers, and time; a dimension of performance. *See also* dimensions of performance.

Core competence 1) A social unit's collective knowledge about how to coordinate diverse production skills and technologies. 2) A primary area of expertise that distinguishes one social unit from others by providing value to users. Core competencies and the network of integrated processes that comprise them are so important to social units that they form the basis for ongoing performance measurement and improvement activities. *See also* core process; hazard analysis; rehearsal; surveillance; warning; logistics.

Core outcome The cumulative effect at a defined point in time of performing one or more core processes. *See* core process; outcome.

Core process An interrelated series of activities, actions, events, mechanisms, or steps that transform inputs into outputs for a particular beneficiary or customer; core processes comprise core competencies. *See also* core competence; core outcome; process.

CQI Continuous quality improvement. *See* performance management.

Curve, bell-shaped *See* bell-shaped curve.

Data The collection of material or facts on which a discussion or an inference is based; data are the product of measurement. Strictly speaking, the word "data" is the plural of "datum." Nevertheless, the two words are used interchangeably in conventional writing and speaking today. *See also* information.

Data accuracy The degree to which data is free of errors or mistakes. *See also* data.

Database An organized collection of data, text, references, or pictures in a standardized format, typically stored in a computer system so that any particular item or set of items can be extracted or organized as needed. Databases may vary in content, type of information contained, and design. *See also* data; data set.

Data collection The process of gathering materials or facts on how a process works. *See also* data.

Data, continuous *See* continuous data.

Data element A discrete piece of data. Data elements may be aggregated with other data elements to identify occurrences of an indicator event targeted for measurement. *See also* data; indicator.

Data interpretation The multi-step process by which meaning is assigned to raw data.

Data, measurement *See* measurement data.

Data pattern An identifiable arrangement of data that suggests a systematic design or orderly formation relative to a data set. *See also* data.

Data reliability The degree to which data resulting from a data-collection process is accurate and complete. *See also* data validity; indicator reliability; reliability.

Data set An aggregation of uniformly defined and classified data or items of information that describe an element, episode, or aspect of an area. *See also* data; database.

Data trend One type of data pattern consisting of the general direction of data measurements; for example, a trend on a run chart or control chart is the continued rise or fall of a series of points. *See also* pattern; trend.

Data validity The degree to which data is a reasonable representation of the phenomenon it is collected to measure. *See also* data reliability; indicator validity.

Demand management In the context of disaster preparedness, the totality of goal-directed measures that influence a condition requiring relief; one of the three main processes comprising logistics. *See also* supply management, fulfillment management.

Desirable indicator An outcome or process indicator that measures a desirable outcome or process. *See also* indicator.

Detectability, hazard *See* hazard detectability.

Deviation, standard *See* standard deviation.

Dimensions of performance Characteristics of performance that are related to "doing the right things" and "doing things well." Performance dimensions are definable, measurable, and improvable. *See also* appropriateness; availability; coordination; effectiveness; efficacy, efficiency; private citizen perspective issues; safety; timeliness.

Disaster A state or condition destabilizing a social system. Disaster manifests itself in the malfunctioning, disruption, or partial or total destruction of connections and communications between the elements of the social system. Disasters require extraordinary countermeasures to reestablish stability. *See also* disaster preparedness.

Disaster agent A class or category of phenomena that cause disasters, such as hurricanes, tornadoes, or explosions. *See also* disaster; hazard.

Disaster cycle An explicit typology for disaster planning, comprised of four phases: mitigation, preparedness, response, recovery. *See also* disaster; mitigation, preparedness, response, recovery.

Disaster drill *See* rehearsal.

Disaster exercise *See* rehearsal.

Disaster, natural *See* natural disaster.

Disaster preparedness The totality of goal-directed measures undertaken in anticipation of disaster. *See also* disaster; preparedness.

Disaster, technological *See* technological disaster.

Discrete data Data that can be arranged into naturally occurring or arbitrarily selected groups or sets of values, as opposed to continuous data, which have no naturally occurring breaks. *Compare* continuous data. *See also* data; discrete variable.

Discrete variable A measurement that is limited to discrete options (e.g., yes/no/ unknown). *Compare* continuous variable. *See also* discrete data.

Discrete variable indicator *See* rate-based indicator.

Dispersion *See* standard deviation.

Distribution *See* frequency distribution.

Distribution, frequency *See* frequency distribution.

Distribution, normal *See* normal distribution.

Drill *See* rehearsal.

Duration of impact, hazard *See* hazard duration of impact.

Effectiveness The degree to which a process is performed in the correct manner, given the current state of knowledge, to achieve desired outcomes; a dimension of performance. *See also* dimensions of performance.

Efficacy The degree to which a process accomplishes what it is designed to accomplish; a dimension of performance. *See also* dimensions of performance.

Efficiency The ratio of the results of a process to the resources used to perform the process; a dimension of performance. *See also* dimensions of performance.

Emergency-operations center (EOC) The physical location where leaders meet to make policy and strategic management decisions during a disaster or disaster exercise. *See also* emergency-operations plan.

Emergency-operations plan (EOP) The written plan of a political subdivision describing the organization, mission, and functions of the political subdivision government and supporting services for responding to and recovering from disasters. *See also* emergency-operations center.

EOC *See* emergency-operations center.

EOP *See* emergency-operations plan.

Endogenous cause *See* common cause.

Endogenous-cause variation *See* common-cause variation.

Exercise *See* rehearsal.

Exercise, full-scale *See* full-scale exercise.

Exercise, functional *See* functional exercise.

Exogenous cause *See* special cause.

Face validity Intelligibility; the degree to which a measure or test makes sense to an informed user. Face validity is the most superficial type of validity; nevertheless, it often contributes to the presumed legitimacy of an indicator and is, therefore, an important consideration in gaining acceptance of an indicator. *See also* validity.

Facility, chemical *See* chemical facility.

Fishbone diagram *See* cause-and-effect diagram.

Flowchart (flow chart) A pictorial summary that shows with symbols and words the steps, sequence, and relationship of the various operations involved in the performance of a process.

Frequency distribution In statistics, the complete summary of the frequencies of the values or categories of measurement made on a group of entities. The distribution tells either how many or what proportion of the group was found to have each value (or each range of values) out of all the possible values that the quantitative measure may have. A bell-shaped curve (called also a normal distribution) is an example of a distribution in which the greatest number of observations fall in the center, with fewer and fewer observations falling evenly on either side of the average. *Synonym*: distribution. *See also* normal distribution.

Fulfillment management The transportation, distribution, and warehousing of supplies to end users; one of the three main processes comprising logistics. *See also* demand management, supply management.

Function A goal-directed interrelated group of processes. *See also* process.

Functional exercise A time-pressured exercise of a minimum number of functions of an emergency-operations plan, involving strategic and tactical decision making, including the direction and control function, activating the emergency operations center or the incident command post, or both. *See also* emergency operations center; emergency operations plan; full-scale exercise; rehearsal; tabletop exercise.

Full-scale exercise A time-pressured exercise of a minimum number of functions of an emergency-operations plan, involving strategic and tactical decision making, including the direction and control function, activating the emergency operations center and incident command post and deploying responders, equipment, and resources to the field. *See also* functional exercise; rehearsal; tabletop exercise.

Guideline Standardized specifications for processes developed by a formal process that incorporates the best scientific evidence of effectiveness with expert opinion. *See also* standard.

Hazard An extreme phenomenon that has the potential to harm human settlements. *See also* disaster.

Hazard analysis The process of quantifying the probability that extreme events will harm human settlements in a given geographic area during a specified time interval; comprised of three components: hazard identification, vulnerability assessment, and risk analysis. *See also* core process; hazard; hazard identification; risk analysis; vulnerability assessment.

Hazard certainty The level of confidence that predications and detections will be accurate and not result in false alarms. *See also* hazard.

Hazard, complex *See* complex hazard.

Hazard detectability The degree to which predictions correlate well with the impacts that actually occur. *See also* hazard.

Hazard duration of impact The time between the beginning and ending of hazard impacts in which warning information can be disseminated. *See also* hazard.

Hazard identification The process of identifying what hazards have threatened a community, how often specified hazards have occurred in the past, and with what intensity (i.e., damage-generating attributes measured by various scales) they have struck; the first level of hazard analysis sophistication. *See also* hazard analysis.

Hazard lead time The amount of time between prediction/detection and the impact of the hazard. *See also* hazard.

Hazard, manmade *See* technological hazard.

Hazard, natural *See* natural hazard.

Hazardous Involving risk or danger. *See also* hazardous material.

Hazardous Material (HAZMAT) Any material which is explosive, flammable, poisonous, corrosive, reactive, or radioactive (or any combination) and requires special care in handling because of the hazards posed to public health, safety, and/or the environment. *See also* chemical; hazard.

Hazard predictability The degree to which a hazard can be forecasted well with respect to magnitude, location, and timing.

Hazard risk The probability that a hazard event will occur within a specified time interval; the third and highest level of hazard analysis sophistication. *See also* hazard analysis.

Hazard, technological *See* technological hazard.

Hazard visibility The degree to which the hazard physically manifests itself so that it can be seen or otherwise sensed. *See also* hazard.

HAZMAT *See* hazardous material.

HEICS *See* Hospital Emergency Incident Command System.

Hospital Emergency Incident Command System (HEICS) An application of the Incident Command System to the hospital setting. *See also* Incident Command System.

Humanitarian logistics The processes and systems involved in mobilizing people, resources, skills, and knowledge to help vulnerable people affected by disasters. *See also* logistics.

ICS *See* Incident Command System.

Improvement, performance *See* performance improvement.

Incident Command System (ICS) A centralized, hierarchical, and standardized on-scene emergency-management concept specifically designed to allow its users to adopt an integrated organization structure equal to the complexity and demands of single or multiple incidents without being hindered by jurisdictional boundaries. *See also* Hospital Emergency Incident Command System.

Indicator A measurement tool used to quantify performance of processes and achievement of outcomes. Indicators are not direct measures of performance. Rather, they are neutral screens that raise important performance questions that may lead to identification of governance, managerial, provider, and/or support processes in which opportunities for improvement exist. *See also* process; outcome.

Indicator, aggregate data *See* aggregate data indicator.

Indicator data collection logic An indicator information set component that describes the sequence of data element retrieval and aggregation through which numerator events and denominator events are identified by an indicator. *See also* indicator information set.

Indicator definition of terms An indicator information set component that explains terms used in the indicator statement. *See also* indicator information set.

Indicator, desirable *See* desirable indicator.

Indicator development form A form used to describe and record the development process for an individual indicator. *See also* indicator; indicator information set.

Indicator, discrete variable *See* rate-based indicator.

Indicator information set Indicator-specific information typically composed of an indicator statement, definition of terms, indicator type, rationale, description of indicator population, indicator data collection logic, and underlying factors that may explain variation sin data. *See also* indicator.

Indicator population An indicator information set component that describes an indicator's numerator and denominator; populations may be subcategorized to provide more homogeneous populations for subsequent data assessment. *See also* indicator information set.

Indicator, rate-based *See* rate-based indicator.

Indicator rationale An indicator information set component that explains why an indicator is useful in specifying and assessing the process or outcome measured by the indicator. *See also* indicator information set.

Indicator reliability The degree to which an indicator accurately and completely identifies occurrences from among all cases at risk of being indicator occurrences. *See also* data reliability; indicator validity; reliability.

Indicator, sentinel event *See* sentinel event indicator.

Indicator underlying factors Indicator information set component that delineates citizen-, provider-, organizational-, community-, state-, and federal-level factors that may explain variation in performance data and thereby direct performance improvement activities and efforts. *See also* indicator information set.

Indicator validity The degree to which an indicator identifies events that merit further review by various individuals or groups, providing or in some way influencing the process or outcome defined by the indicator. *See also* data validity; indicator reliability; validity.

Information Data that have been transformed through analysis and interpretation into a form useful for drawing conclusions and making decisions. *See also* data.

Inspection Activities, such as measuring, examining, testing, or gauging one or more characteristics of a product or service and comparing these with specified requirements to determine conformity. Inspection is a past-oriented strategy that attempts to identify unacceptable output after it has been produced and separate it from the good output.

Interpretation The process of explaining the meaning of.

Interquartile range A measure of the dispersion around the median of a distribution; useful in skewed frequency distributions. *See also* frequency distribution.

Ishikawa diagram *See* cause-and-effect diagram.

Lead time, hazard *See* hazard lead time.

Logistics The totality of resource mobilization measures undertaken in anticipation of imminent disaster. *See also* core process; disaster preparedness; preparedness.

Logistics, humanitarian *See* humanitarian logistics.

Lower control limit *See* control limit.

Maximum threat The "worst-case scenario," meaning the worst conceivable destruction of life and property that a hazard could cause. *See also* hazard; hazard analysis.

Mean A measure of central tendency of a collection of data specifying the arithmetic average. A mean consists of the sum of all the measurements of the data set divided by the total number of measures in the data set. The mean is best used when the distribution of data is balanced and unimodal. In a normal distribution, the mean coincides with the median and mode. *Synonym*: average. *See also* median; mode; measures of central tendency; frequency distribution; normal distribution.

Measurable Capable of being quantified, as in measurable performance. *See also* measure.

Measure 1) A quantitative tool or instrument used to make measurements, as in an indicator. 2) A unit specified by a measurement scale.

Measurement 1) The process of quantification, that is, determining that attribute of a person, an activity, or a thing by which it is greater or less than some other person, activity, or thing. 2) The number resulting from a quantification process. *See also* performance measurement.

Measurement data Data resulting from quantifying attributes or characteristics of person, activities, or things. *See also* measurement.

Measurement, performance *See* performance measurement.

Measure, performance Any instrument, such as an indicator, for quantifying levels of performance. *See* also measure; performance; performance measurement.

Measures of central tendency Several characteristics of the distribution of a set of measurements around a value or values at or near the middle of the set. The principal measures of central tendency are the mean, median, and mode. *See also* mean; median; mode.

Mitigation The totality of measures undertaken at a time distant from an actual disaster situation to permanently prevent or reduce future disaster impact (e.g., building codes and land-use regulations). *See also* disaster cycle.

Mode A measure of central tendency of a collection of data, consisting of the measurement of the data set that occurs most often. *See also* mean; median; measures of central tendency.

Monitor Measure over time.

Natural disaster Any hurricane, tornado, storm, flood, high water, wind-driven water, tidal wave, tsunami, earthquake, volcanic eruption, landslide, mudslide, snowstorm, drought, fire, or other catastrophe in any part of the United States that causes, or that may cause, substantial damage or injury to civilian property or persons. (Robert T. Stafford Act, 602.) *See also* disaster.

Natural hazard A naturally-occurring phenomenon that puts life or property at risk. *See also* hazard.

Norm 1) The *average* or *usual* numerical level or pattern at which an action, event, or other measured phenomenon occurs within a defined population. 2) A numerical level of a *desired* action, event, or other measured phenomenon. *See also* normal distribution.

Normal distribution A frequency distribution that is continuous and symmetrical with both tails of the distribution, extending to infinity. The arithmetic mean, mode, and median are identical, and the shape of the distribution is completely determined by the mean and standard deviation. *Synonym*: bell-shaped curve. *See also* frequency distribution.

One-Hundred-Year Floodplain The land area adjoining a river, stream, lake, or ocean which is inundated by the one-hundred-year flood, also referred to as a flood having a one percent chance of occurring in any given year. The one-hundred-year flood is the regulatory (base) flood under the National Flood Insurance Program.

Outcome The cumulative effect at a defined point in time of performing one or more processes. *See also* core outcome; outcome indicator; process.

Outcome, core *See* core outcome.

Outcome indicator An indicator that measures what happens or does not happen, depending on the degree to which one or more processes are performed well. *See also* indicator; outcome; process indicator.

Pareto chart A special form of vertical bar graph that displays information in such a way that priorities for process improvements can be established. It displays the relative importance of all the data and is used to direct efforts to the largest improvement opportunity by highlighting the vital few in contrast to the many others.

Pattern A particular design or arrangement. *See also* trend.

Performance Something that is done before an audience. Performance can be quantitatively measured and then compared with other similar measurements. Accurate, complete, and relevant performance data can provider users with *objective* evidence upon which judgments can be based. *See also* quality.

Performance assessment The analysis and interpretation of performance-measurement data to transform it into useful information; the second component of performance management. The product of performance assessment is information. *See also* assessment; performance; performance management.

Performance data Data that provide information about performance, as in disaster-preparedness performance data. *See also* data.

Performance dimensions *See* dimensions of performance.

Performance improvement The continuous study and adjustment of processes to increase the probability of achieving desired outcomes; the third component of performance-management. *See* also performance; performance management.

Performance indicator An instrument that measures performance. *See also* indicator.

Performance management A framework that identifies opportunities for performance improvement through use of performance measures such as indicators; comprised of three components: performance measurement, performance assessment, and performance improvement. Synonyms and near synonyms include continuous quality improvement (CQI), quality improvement (QI), continuous improvement (CI), total quality management (TQM), performance improvement (PI), and continuous performance improvement (CPI), among others. *See also* performance assessment; performance improvement; performance measurement.

Performance measure Any instrument (such as an indicator) for quantifying levels of performance. *See also* measure; performance; performance measurement.

Performance measurement The quantification of processes and outcomes using one or more dimensions of performance, such as efficiency or effectiveness. Performance measurement is the first component of performance measurement, performance assessment, and performance improvement. *See also* performance; performance assessment; performance improvement.

Predictability, hazard *See* hazard predictability.

Preparedness The totality of measures undertaken in anticipation of imminent disaster (e.g., hazard analysis, surveillance, warning, logistics). *See also* disaster preparedness; logistics; mitigation; recovery; response.

Private citizen perspective issues The degree to which individuals who live or work in a community are involved in the decision-making process in matters pertaining to disaster preparedness and the degree to which they are satisfied with the disaster-preparedness services that they receive; a dimension of performance.

Process An interrelated series of activities, actions, events, mechanisms, or steps that transform inputs into outputs for a particular beneficiary or customer. *See also* process indicator; outcome.

Process indicator An indicator that measures an interrelated series of activities, actions, events, mechanisms, or steps that transforms inputs into outputs for a particular beneficiary or customer. The best process indicators focus on processes that are closely linked to outcomes, meaning that a scientific basis exists for believing that the process, when performed well, will increase the probability of achieving a desired outcome. *See also* indicator; outcome indicator.

Process standard A standard that identifies activities that should or should not be done. *See also* process.

Process variation The spread of process output over time. There is variation in every process, and all variation is caused. The causes are of two types: special or common. A process can have both types of variation at the same time or only common-cause variation. The management action necessary to improve the process varies depending on the type of variation being addressed. *See also* commoncause variation; special-cause variation; variation.

Proportion A type of ratio in which the numerator is expressed as a subset of the denominator. *See also* ratio.

Quality A judgment proceeding from or taking place in a person's mind rather than in the external world. *See also* performance.

Range In statistics, a measure of the variation in a set of data calculated by subtracting the lowest value in the data set from the highest value in that same set. *See also* standard deviation.

Range, interquartile *See* interquartile range.

Rate-based indicator An aggregate data indicator in which the value of each measurement is expressed as a proportion or as a ratio. *Synonym*: discrete variable indicator. *See also* aggregate data indicator; indicator; proportion; ratio.

Ratio The relationship between two quantities when the numerator and denominator measure different phenomena. *Compare* proportion.

Recovery The totality of post-response measures undertaken to restore normalcy (e.g., rebuilding homes and reopening local businesses). *See also* disaster cycle.

Rehearsal The process of simulating a disaster for the purpose of measuring, assessing, and improving a social unit's future performance in a real disaster. *See also* core process; disaster; disaster preparedness.

Reliability 1) The ability of an item to perform a required function under stated conditions. 2) In performance measurement, consistency in results of a measure, including the tendency of the measure to produce the same results twice when it measures some entity or attribute believed not to have changed in the interval between measurements. 3) Statistically, reliability refers to the degree to which scores are free from random error. *See also* data reliability; indicator reliability.

Resilience The degree to which a community can recover successfully ("bounce back") from loss and damage. Elements of community resilience include the totality of measures undertaken by communities *in anticipation* of disaster (i.e., disaster preparedness measures). *See also* disaster preparedness; vulnerability.

Response The totality of measures undertaken during and immediately after disaster impact to resolve to the degree possible crisis-time problems (e.g., damage assessment, debris removal, search and rescue efforts, emergency medical services). *See also* disaster cycle.

Risk, hazard *See* hazard risk.

Run chart A display of data in which data points are plotted as they occur over time to detect trends or other patterns and variation occurring over time. *Compare* control chart.

Safety The degree to which the hazard risk in the environment is reduced for private citizens, providers, organizations, and the community; a dimension of performance.

Saffir/Simpson scale A scale for expressing the relative intensity of hurricanes, consisting of five levels of increasing intensity—that is, Categories 1 through 5.

Sentinel event In performance measurement, a serious event that triggers further investigation each time it occurs. *See also* sentinel event indicator.

Sentinel event indicator A type of indicator that identifies an individual event or phenomenon that triggers further analysis and investigation each time it occurs. *See also* aggregate data indicator; sentinel event.

Special cause A factor that intermittently and unpredictably induces variation over and above that inherent in the system. It often appears as an extreme point, such a point beyond the control limits on a control chart. *Synonyms*: assignable cause; exogenous cause; extrasystemic cause. *Compare* common cause. *See also* control chart; special-cause variation; variation.

Special-cause variation The variation in performance and data that results from special causes. Special-cause variation is intermittent, unpredictable, and unstable. It is not inherently present in a system; rather, it arises from causes that are not part of the system as designed. It tends to cluster by person, place, and time. *Synonyms*: assignable-cause variation; exogenous-cause variation; extrasystemic-cause variation. *Compare*: common-cause variation. *See also* process variation; special cause; tampering; variation.

Spread *See* standard deviation.

Standard Statement of expectations that defines a social unit's capacity to perform processes well and achieve desired outcomes. A standard may be used as a criterion or acknowledged measure of comparison for quantitative or qualitative value. Conformity or compliance with standards is usually a condition of licensure, certification, and accreditation. *See also* guideline; measure.

Standard, structural *See* structural standard.

Standard deviation (SD) A measure of variability that indicates the dispersion, spread, or variation in a distribution. *Compare* range.

Standard, process *See* process standard.

Standards-based review Approach to performance measurement that uses pre-established structure- and process-oriented standards to focus attention on the factors that must exist to perform processes well and achieve desired outcomes. *See also* case-based review; standard.

Standard, structural *See* structural standard.

Statistical control The condition describing a process from which all special causes have been removed, evidenced on a control chart by the absence of points beyond the control limits and by the absence of nonrandom patterns or trends within the control limits. *See also* control; control chart; control limit; special cause.

Structural standard A standard that pertains to the type, number, and characteristics of the resources of a social unit. *See also* standard.

Supply management The procurement of supplies, production planning, and inventory; one of the three main processes comprising logistics. *See* also demand management, fulfillment management.

Surge capability *See* surge capacity.

Surge capacity A community's potential to respond effectively and efficiently to a sudden, transient increase in demand for specified requirements, such as water and hospital services.

Surveillance: The process of collecting, collating, and interpreting data to produce useful information. *See also* core process; disaster.

Tabletop exercise: A low-stress, non-time-pressured, discussion-based exercise of a minimum number of functions of the emergency-operations plan, including the direction-and-control function, held in the emergency-operations center, the incident-command post or another suitable facility. See also function; functional exercise; full-scale exercise; rehearsal.

Tampering In data analysis, the act of taking action on some signal of variation without taking into account the difference between special-cause and common-cause variation. *See also* common-cause variation; special-cause variation.

Technological disaster Social disruption caused by manmade systems. *See also* disaster.

Technological hazard A hazard caused by manmade systems. *See also* complex hazard; natural hazard.

Timeliness The degree to which a process is performed at the time it is most beneficial or necessary; a dimension of performance.

TOPOFF 1 A U.S. Congress-mandated counterterrorism full-scale exercise in May 2000 that took place in Denver, Colorado, and Portsmouth, New Hampshire. In 1998, Congress directed the attorney general and the director of Federal Emergency Management Agency to undertake a full-scale exercise that involved federal agency personnel and state and local emergency responders, including law enforcement, fire, and emergency medical personnel, who participated in the crisis and consequence management of a domestic weapons-of-mass-destruction terrorist attack. The goal of the exercise, called "TOPOFF" because of the involvement of top officials, was to assess the nation's crisis and consequence management capacity under extraordinarily stressful conditions. *See also* full-scale exercise; rehearsal; TOPOFF 2; weapons of mass destruction.

TOPOFF 2 A U.S. Congress-mandated full-scale counterterrorism exercise in May 2003 that took place in Chicago and Seattle metropolitan areas. In 1998, Congress directed the attorney general and the director of Federal Emergency Management Agency to undertake a full-scale exercise that involved federal agency personnel and state and local emergency responders, including law enforcement, fire and emergency medical personnel, who participated in the crisis and consequence management of a domestic weapons-of-mass-destruction terrorist attack. The State of Washington, King County, and the City of Seattle responded to a hypothetical explosion containing radioactive material. The State of Illinois, Cook, Lake, DuPage and Kane Counties, and the City of Chicago responded to a covert release of a biological agent. Nineteen federal agencies and the American Red Cross were involved during the five-day exercise. The National Capital Region, including the District of Columbia, State of Maryland, and

Commonwealth of Virginia, participated in the first day of the exercise. *See also* full-scale exercise; rehearsal; TOPOFF 1; weapons of mass destruction.

TQM Total quality management. *See* performance management.

Trend Any general direction of movement. A trend, although possibly irregular in the short time, shows movement consistently in the same direction over a longer term. *See also* data trend.

Upper control limit *See* control limit.

Validity The degree to which an observed situation reflects the true situation. In performance measurement, the degree to which an indicator identifies an event that merits further review by various individuals or groups providing or affecting the process or outcome defined by the indicator. *See also* face validity; indicator validity.

Validity, face *See* face validity.

Variation The inevitable difference among individual outputs of a processes; excessive variation frequently leads to waste and loss. The sources of variation derive from common causes and special causes. *See also* common cause; process variation; special cause.

Variation, common cause *See* common-cause variation.

Variation, process *See* process variation.

Variation, special cause *See* special-cause variation.

Visibility, hazard *See* hazard visibility.

Vulnerability assessment The process of quantifying the susceptibility of human settlements to the harmful impacts of hazards, including human deaths and injuries, property damage, and indirect losses, such as interruption of business and production; the second level of hazard analysis sophistication. *See also* assessment; hazard analysis; hazard identification; risk analysis.

Warning The process of detecting imminent disaster and distributing that information to people at risk. *See also* core process.

Weapons of mass destruction (WMD) In arms-control usage, nuclear, chemi-cal, biological and radiological weapons that are capable of a high order of destruction and of being used in such a manner as to destroy large numbers of people. *Synonym*: WMD.

WMD *See* weapons of mass destruction.

Worst-case-scenario *See* maximum threat.

Index

A

aggregate data indicator 49, 52-54
  defined 52, 119
  vs. sentinel event indicator 52
Alexander the Great 19
all-hazards approach 119
American Red Cross 57
algorithm 41
anthrax 56
appropriateness 50, 51, 119
Army Corps of Engineers 14
assessment 119
availability 50, 51, 119
average 119

B

bell-shaped curve 84, 86, 120
Bell Telephone 100
benchmark, defined 32, 120
benchmarking 32, 120
Bhopal, India 2
Bice, Steven 21
bomb technician 48, 98
Bradford Hill 33
brainstorming 114, 120
building codes 1

C

case-based review 37, 39, 120
cause-and-effect diagram 114, 120
center line 120
Centers for Disease Control and Prevention 20
  and Steven Bice 21
  and Strategic National Stockpile 21
  and smallpox vaccine 20
central tendency 86
CERT 63
certainty 15
checksheet 114, 120
chemical 120
  facility 120
citizens 50
Civil Defense Warning System 15
Clackamas County (Oregon) 7, 8, 11, 12, 17
  and emergency levels 8
Claypool, Robert 21
common cause 100, 121
  variation 101, 121
community
  commitment to disaster preparedness 2
  defined 2-3, 121
complex
  disaster 3, 121
  hazard 121
computer intrusion 48
continuous
  data 54, 121
  variable 54, 55, 122
  variable data 55
  variable indicator 49, 54, 55, 60, 122
control 122
  chart 100, 104-108, 122
  limit 122
coordination 50, 51, 122
core competence 4-5, 122
  defined 5

of 3M 5
of emergency medicine 5
of law enforcement 5
core outcome 123
core process
    defined 5, 123
    of disaster preparedness 5-22

D
damage assessment 1
data
    accuracy 123
    collection 123
    collection logic 62
    continuous 54
    defined 123
    discrete 54
    element 123
    interpretation 123
    parsimony 75
    pattern 123
    reliability 124
    set 124
    trend 124
    tampering 103
    validity 124
    variation 100-111
database 40, 123
debris removal 1
demand management 19, 20, 124
desirable indicator 49, 50, 124
detectability 15, 128
dimensions of performance 50-52, 124
disaster
    agent, defined 3, 124
    complex 3
    cycle 1-2, 124
    defined 2-3, 124
    drills See rehearsals

exercises See rehearsals
functions 17
manmade 3,
mitigation 1, 132
natural 3, 132
preparedness
    and rehearsals 17-18
    defined 1, 2, 125, 135
recovery 2, 136
resilience 5
response 1, 136
discrete
    data 54, 125
    indicator 49
    variable 53, 54, 125
    variable data 54
    variable indicator 54, 60
dispersion 90, 91
Doppler radar 15
doxycycline 21
duration of impact 15

E
effectiveness 50, 51, 125
efficacy 50, 51, 126
efficiency 50, 51, 126
Emergency Alert System 15
emergency department 41
emergency medical services 1
emergency medical technician (EMT) 41, 42
emergency-operations center 29, 126
emergency-operations plan 17, 38, 126
    defined 17
emergency services and disaster agency (ESDA) 38
emergent organizations 3
Environmental Protection Agency See U.S. Environmental Protection Agency
exercises See rehearsals

expert
content 70
methodology 70

F
face validity 56-57, 126
factors
community 63
organization 63
influencing variation 112-116
private citizen 63, 80
provider 63
state and federal 63, 80
fire department 25
firefighters 50
and Phoenix, Arizona 41
first responder 51, 62
flash flood warning lead time 105, 107, 113
flood insurance 54
floodplain, one-hundred year 133
floodplain resident 54
flowchart 114, 127
frequency distribution 82-99, 127
fulfillment management 19, 21-22, 127
full-scale exercise 38, 40
defined 18, 127
functional exercise 18, 38, 127
function, defined 17, 127

G
governance 40
Great Midwest Flood of 1993 14
guideline 40, 41, 127

H
Hamel 4-5
hazard
analysis See hazard analysis
certainty 128
defined 3, 127
detectability 128
duration of impact 128
identification 6-7, 128
lead time 128
natural 3, 133
predictability 128
probabilities 12
ranking list
Clackamas County (Oregon) 12
Kane County (Illinois) 10
risk 129
technologic 3
hazard analysis 1, 5-13, 38, 128
criteria, Clackamas County (Oregon) 11
hazardous materials 8, 9, 10, 16, 50, 51, 101, 128
hazardous surveillance See surveillance
Homeland Security Advisory System 16
Hospital Emergency Incident Command System 4
humanitarian relief organizations 19
and logistics 129
hurricane 12, 16

I
Idaho State Communications Center 91, 102
Illinois Emergency Management Agency
Act 37,
and ESDA 38
incident command system 129
hospital 4, 129
and indicators 43
indicator
aggregate data 49
as part of performance-measurement framework 39, 40
characteristics of 47-68
continuous variable 49
data collection logic 57, 58, 62, 130
data frequency distribution 82

defined 40, 129, 134
definition of terms 57, 58, 59, 130
desirable 49, 50
development form 64-66, 130
development process 69-76
discrete variable 49
information set 57-61, 130
outcome 47, 49
parsimony 75
population 57, 58, 130
process 47, 49
rate-based 49
rationale 57, 58, 60, 65, 130
reliability 56-57, 77-81, 130
sentinel event 49
statement 57, 58, 59
testing process 77-81
typology 57, 58, 59-60
underlying factors 58, 62, 66, 130
undesirable 49
validity 56-57, 77-82, 130
vs. guidelines/standards 41
information
  defined 13, 131
  set, indicator 57-61
inspection 131
International Red Cross 19
interquartile range 91, 95-96, 131
Ishikawa 115, 131

K
Kane County (Illinois) 9, 10

L
land-use regulations 1
lead time 15
LEPC See local emergency-planning committee
local emergency-planning committee 2
logistics 1, 5, 6, 19-22

and demand management 19, 20, 124
and fulfillment management 19, 21-22, 127
and humanitarian relief 129
and supply management 19, 21
and surge capacity 20
defined 19, 131
humanitarian 19-21
tyranny of 19

M
maximum threat 131
mean 87, 89, 131
measurable 132
measure 132
measurement
  barriers to 32
  benefits of 32-33
  data 132
  defined 31-32, 132
median 87, 89
mesocyclone 15
mitigation See disaster
mode 88, 89, 132
monitor 132

N
National Primary Drinking Water Regulations 41
National Hurricane Center 16
National Oceanic and
  Atmospheric Administration 15
National Storm Center 15
National Weather Service 14, 15
natural disaster See disaster
New York City 29
NOAA See National Oceanic
and Atmospheric Administration 15
norm 133
normal distribution 133

O

one-hundred year floodplain 133
Oxfam 19
outcome 133
   indicator 49

P

Pareto chart 114, 133
pattern 133
performance
   assessment 30,
      defined 31, 134
   data 134
   database 43
   defined 30, 134
   dimensions of 50-52, 134
   improvement 31, 112
      defined 31, 134
   indicators See Indicators
   management 29-36, 134
   measure 134
   measurement 1, 30, 134
      and database 39
      and guidelines/standards 39
      and indicators 39, 40
      framework of 37-46
      defined 31
   variations 1
   vs. quality, defined 30
PET 2
pharmaceutical vendors 42
Phoenix, Arizona 41
   and guidelines 41
Plainfield (Illinois) 15
police department 25
policies 41
Prahalad 4-5
predictability 14, 128
preparedness See disaster

private citizen perspective issues 50, 52, 63, 135
procedures 41
process
   average 112
   defined 5, 135
   indicator 49, 135
   standard, defined 38, 135
   variation 135
process, core See core process
proportion 54, 135
Public Water System Supervision program 41
public works 17
push packages 21

Q

quality, defined 30, 136
   vs. performance, defined 30

R

range 90, 91, 135
rate-based indicator 49, 54, 55, 136
ratio 54, 136
rationale, indicator See indicator
recovery See Disaster
Red Cross See International Red Cross
rehearsals 1, 5, 6, 16-19
   defined 16, 136
      full-scale exercise, defined 18
      functional exercise, defined 18
      tabletop exercise, defined 17
reliability 136
resilience 136
response See Disaster
risk analysis 6, 11-13, 129
Rosen Dennis 34
run chart 137

S

safety 50, 52, 137

Saffir/Simpson scale 12, 137
search and rescue 1
sentinel event 137
    indicator 49, 52, 55-56, 137
Shewhart, Walter 100
    and control charts 104
skewed 89
smallpox
    and first responder 60
    vaccine 20, 21, 22
        and adverse reaction 49, 51
special cause 100, 137
    variation 101, 137
standard
    defined 37, 40, 41, 137
    process 38-39
    structural 37-38, 138
standard deviation 91, 138
standards-based review 37-38, 138
statistical control 138
statistics 34
stockpile See Strategic National Stockpile
Strategic National Stockpile 21, 40, 42, 47
    deployment lead time 40, 49, 51
structural standard See standard
surge capability 20, 138
surge capacity 20, 138
surveillance 1, 5, 6, 13-14, 50
    defined 138
    and quality dimension 13-14
    and spatial dimension 13
    and time dimension 13

T
tabletop exercise 17-18, 38, 138
tampering 103, 139
technological
    disaster 139
    hazard 139

terrorist act/attack 20, 49, 55
timeliness 50, 52, 139
TOPOFF 1 139
TOPOFF 2 139
tornado
    and Will County 15
    warning lead time 49, 51, 82, 83, 84, 85, 101
    warning system 15, 33, 55
trend 140

U
underlying factors, indicator See indicator
undesirable indicator 49, 50
Union Carbide Corporation 2
U.S. Department of Defense 42
U.S. Department of Health and Human Services 20
U.S. Department of Homeland Security 16
U.S. Department of Veterans Affairs 21
U.S. Environmental Protection Agency 41, 92, 94
U.S. Governors' Association 1

V
validity, indicator 56-57
    face 56
    defined 140
variation 140
    common-cause 101
    data 100-111
    process 135
    special-cause 101
visibility 15, 129
vulnerability assessment 6, 9-11
    defined 6, 9, 140

W
warning 1, 5, 6, 14-16, 141
weapons of mass destruction 141
Weather Radio 15

Western Electric Company 100
Whitaker 1
Will County (Illinois) 15
World Trade Center 29

Y

Y2K 18-19

0-595-31708-1

Printed in the United States
60439LVS00003B/155